CONTENTS

Introduction

History is horrible. For a start, everybody in history is dead. Some are very dead indeed.

Of course history teachers don't tell you this, do they?

And then teacher drones on about boring battles and dusty dates. What you really want to know is the really interesting stuff. How did people live ... and how did they die?

For example, teacher may tell you that in the age of King George III, Britain won the Battle of Waterloo (thanks to a man in Wellington's boots). But you really want to know about what happened *after* the battle, don't you? When people went over the battlefield looking in the mouths of the corpses for nice, shiny teeth. And, when they found them, they pulled them out.

Could you rip teeth out of a fresh corpse? Probably not. So why did the tooth collectors of Waterloo? For money!

No, stupid, they didn't put them under their pillows and wait for the tooth fairy. They sold them to people who made sets of false teeth.

Could you wear false teeth knowing they'd been picked from a variety of dead bodies?

See? The Battle of Waterloo is just an important date to remember for a history teacher. But it was a good day for business if you were a tooth collector.

There are plenty of books full of dates – they're called diaries. But if you want a bit of real live death then you need a book that tells you all about the horrible side of history.

And it just so happens you are reading one ...

Timeline

1714 Queen Anne of the Stuart family dies. George I comes from Hanover (Germany) to take the English throne. He's not popular, but the other Stuarts are Catholics and most Brits don't want that.

1715 Stuart supporters want James III to rule so they have a rebellion in support of him – these 'Jacobite' rebellions are crushed … for now.

1727 George II comes to the throne when George I has a violent attack of diarrhoea and dies. Pooh!

1745 Bonnie Prince Charlie – the last of the Stuart family – lands in Scotland to claim the throne of Britain in another Jacobite rebellion. The Scottish clans are brutally beaten by the Brit Army.

1750 First organized police force in London – the Bow Street Runners.

1760 George III comes to the throne – and stays for 60 years in sickness and in health.

1770 Captain Cook claims Australia for Britain. He doesn't bother to ask the Aborigines if they want to be British, of course.

1775 American colonies rebel against British rule.

1788 Australia welcomes its first

British convicts. It's a good place to dump them. And only 48 die on the voyage!

1789 The French peasants revolt against their rulers. Soon they'll be slicing noble heads off with the guillotine.

1792 First gas lighting in houses, invented by some bright spark.

1793 The French have chopped their King Louis' head. Now they're looking for a fight and pick on Britain. The start of 20 years of wars – the Napoleonic Wars.

1798 Steam-powered spinning mill opens in Bradford. Bad news for spinners working from home, being replaced by machines. They'll all have to take jobs at the dangerous, dirty factories.

1801 Ireland joins Great Britain and another red cross is added to the flag to make the Union Jack.

1804 Captain Dick's Puffer starts running! The first steam railway locomotive, invented by Richard Trevithick.

1805 British Navy wins Battle of Trafalgar against the French and lose their admiral, Horatio, Lord Nelson, potted by a hot-shot.

1806 Steam-powered looms

8

invented. Bad news for weavers.

1807 Britain bans slave trading – having made a fortune out of it for the past hundred years or so.

1811 Out of work weavers wreck the machines that put them out of work. They call themselves Luddites and male wreckers often dress as women!

1815 Britain defeats Napoleon and his French armies at Waterloo. (A village in Belgium, not a London station.)

1819 It's now against the law for children under nine to work or for older children to work more than 12 hours a day.

1820 Popular (but blind, deaf and mad) George III dies. Unpopular (fat and dishonest) George IV takes over.

1825 First steam-driven passenger railway runs from Stockton to Darlington. Crowds turn up to watch … they are disappointed when it doesn't explode!

1830 Fat George IV dies and his brother, boring William IV, takes over. End of Georgian age.

1837 Queen Victoria comes to the throne. A right madam who will reign even longer than George III.

Gorgeous Georgians

Vicious verses and cruel cartoons

The Georgians could be very cruel to one another. They had their own way of mocking people.

Poets, like Alexander Pope (1688–1744) were especially nasty. (Lady Mary Wortley Montague called him 'the wicked asp of Twickenham'.) His poems poked fun at people but especially people who loved themselves.

Unimportant note 1: The posh word for cruel fun is satire – remember that word!

The other cruel artists were cartoonists. Men like Hogarth (1697-1764) – he made people look ridiculous in his drawings.

Unimportant note 2: The posh word for this is caricature – remember that word too!

Georgian makeover

By the 1770s some of the fashions became quite ridiculous. So here's a *satire* and a *caricature* of ladies' fashion in the age of George III. (And now you can forget those two words. Which two words? Er … I've forgotten.)

Modern magazines offer readers a 'makeover' – they say they'll change someone's appearance from grot to hot in ten easy steps. If the Georgians did a makeover then the results would have been just as stunning …

1. *White is beautiful, dear ladies,*
   Smear your face with paint of lead;
   Never mind the lead has made
   The men who mixed it ill ... or dead.

   ~ Make-up is a flat white lead paint

2. *Take some silk of red or black,*
   Cut a circle or a crescent;
   Stick it to your face to cover
   Smallpox scars ... it's much more pleasant.

   ~Silk beauty spots are cut out and stuck on

3. *Take some plaster, dyed bright red,*
   Crush it to a ruby paste;
   Smear it on your lips, dear ladies,
   Never mind the chalky taste.

   ~Red Plaster of Paris is used for lips

4. *Shave your eyebrows clean away,*
Take a trap and catch some mice;
Make false eyebrows from the mouse skin,
Stick them on to look so nice.

~ Black lead eyelashes and mouse-skin eyebrows are needed

CHEESE MADAM?

YUMMY!

YES PLEASE!

5. *Make your face look sweet and chubby,*
Pack your mouth with balls of cork;
Fit your false teeth in the middle,
Hope you don't choke when you talk.

~ Cork balls held in the cheeks improve the face

BUT MADAM, CRICKET BALLS ARE MADE OF CORK!

6. *Next you need a monster wig*
If you want to look real smashin';
When your wig has reached the ceiling
Then you'll be the height of fashion!

~ Build up the hair like a pyramid

I'M SURE MADAM'S UMBRELLA IS IN THERE SOMEWHERE

7. *Decorate your lovely hairpiece,*
   Use the feathers of a parrot;
   Add some ribbons, fruit and flowers,
   From your ears then hang a carrot.

~Never wear your hair plain

8. *Wear a dress of finest satin,*
   Over wide, hooped petticoats;
   When you walk along the pavement
   Push pedestrians in the road.

~Wide skirts and long trains are the fashion

9. *Don't forget to take your handbag,*
   Fill it with the usual stuff;
   Perfume and sweet vinegar.
   To clear your head you'll need some snuff.

~Fashionable ladies clear their heads with snuff

10. *Last of all you'll need a fan*
To flutter at your favourite feller;
Now you'll look like Ugly Sister
To the pretty Cinderella!

~The finished effect should be a vision of beauty

AAARGH!

Heights of fashion

It wasn't only poets and cartoonists who made fun of ladies. A theatre director called Garrick had a character on stage dressed with every kind of vegetable and a carrot dangling from each ear. Of course real ladies never wore carrots – but they did wear the scarlet flowers of runner beans!

BZZZZZZZZZZZZZZZZZZZZZ........

In 1786 four overdressed ladies were scoffed at as they entered the theatre. Actresses stopped the play and returned wearing similarly ridiculous dress to make fun of the ladies.

In the 1780s the high hair went out of fashion. The writer Addison said …

> *I remember the time when ladies' hair shot up to a great height so that women were so much taller than men. We appeared like grasshoppers beside them. I remember ladies who were once nearly seven feet high and are now a few inches short of five feet.*

Fans were waved in front of the face to keep a lady cool in the steaming hot theatres. Some men complained that the large fans were more like windmills! They were decorated with pictures but also with verses of songs or paragraphs from popular books. (If you got bored at the opera you could always read your fan.) Ladies learned to use fan-fluttering as a signal to people watching. One flutter might mean anger while another flutter might mean love. Fans were also useful to hide a lady's mouth if she had rotten teeth. And they could wave away the foul smell if she had bad breath.

Dresses were worn over wide, hooped petticoats. These came into fashion in 1710 and went out of fashion in 1780 – but at the royal court they were still being worn over 40 years later. A writer complained that when one young lady walked down the street she took up the full width of the pavement.

Did you know ...?

In 1776 a lady made the mistake of wearing a decorated hat in the country. It was covered in fruit and vegetables which were fastened on with metal pins. As she sat down for a picnic a passing cow rushed across to eat the hat. Sadly it ate the metal pins too. One stuck in its throat and the cow died a few hours later.

Gorgeous Georgian men

It's easy to poke fun at Georgian women but the men were just as bad. They were known as *fops*, meaning *posers* (and other ruder words!).

1 From 1660 till 1760 it was the century of the slapheads. Men wore wigs – even when they weren't bald! Wigs were popular until the 1760s. They could be very expensive so they were often stolen. Thieves would ride on the back of a carriage, carefully cut a hole through the back, snatch a wig off the passenger and jump off.

2 But wigs could be nasty, filthy things. Topham Beauclark took pleasure in shaking bugs out of his wig in front of lady friends. Many men shaved their heads so the wigs would fit. If they took the wigs off in the comfort of their own home they wore a night-cap (like Wee Willie Winkie!) to keep their heads warm. Really fashionable men wore a turban!

3 Wigs were held in place with powder (made from flour, nutmeg, starch and, maybe, gold dust). Even when wigs went out of fashion a gentleman would hold his hair in place with powder. Walking behind a gentleman on a windy day could choke you! When Prime Minister Pitt put a tax on hair powder in 1795 men stopped using it.

4 Many fops became very fussy about keeping clean and had regular baths. But the clothes of some men were as bad as the dirty wigs. Chelsea pensioners took lice from their coats and bet on races between them.

5 Umbrellas came into fashion in Stuart times but were more common in gorgeous Georgian days. But men who used umbrellas were jeered at in the street. Even in 1797 they were a rare sight – in Cambridge, there was only one umbrella in the whole town. It was kept in a shop and you could hire it if you were caught in a shower.

6 Rich gentlemen could afford clothes just as gorgeous as the ladies'. Silk or velvet coats could be embroidered with silver thread and trimmed with lace. Gorgeous! But the collars and neck-cloths that became popular in the 1820s were starched and ironed till they were stiff as a board. There were reports that some stiff collars chopped off the ear lobes of the young men who wore them!

7 The three-cornered hat, famous in pictures of highwaymen and pirates, was popular in the 1700s. But towards the end of the century an amazing new fashion appeared. Tall, silk, top hats. (You'll have seen them at weddings perhaps.) But the Georgians were amazed when they first saw them. A writer said, 'Women fainted at the sight, children screamed and dogs yelped.'

8 Fashionable young men of the early 1770s were known as Macaronis. They wore thick white make-up, cheek blusher and lipstick. George IV was especially vain about his appearance. He covered his ruddy face in chalk dust and even used leeches to suck his blood to try to make him pale. George also wore a corset to make his bulging waist thinner but his friend, Beau Brummel, told him his trousers didn't fit anyway. George burst into tears.

9 Beau Brummel himself was a leader of men's fashion in Georgian Britain. He plucked or shaved his face several times every day and used three hairdressers. He refused to wear make-up and bathed regularly ... unlike many of his smelly friends. When he argued with George IV he became unpopular and died mad and penniless.

10 Men changed their shape with padding worn under their clothes. They padded the calves of their legs so they didn't look skinny when they wore tight trousers and put pads on their chests to make them look mightier than Tarzan!

Gorging Georgians

Clever cakes

You've probably heard the rhyme:

> *Pat-a-cake, pat-a-cake baker's man!*
> *Bake me a cake as fast as you can;*
> *Pat it and prick it and mark it with 'B',*
> *Put it in the oven for Baby and me.*

But do you know what 'mark it with "B"' means? No? Ask your teacher. Surprise, surprise, they don't know either.

A Georgian child could have told your teacher that a lot of people cooked over open fires and didn't have ovens. They could roast meat or boil puddings but they couldn't *bake* a cake. So a cook would mix a cake and take it to the local baker to bake in his oven. They didn't want their cake mixed up with someone else's, so they marked it with their initial … 'B' for 'baby' in this case.

If your name was Sarah Isobel Catherine King, or Benjamin Uriah Morton, or even Philip Oliver Nigel George Young, then you wouldn't want all of your initials on the cake – would you?

And cake was eaten at breakfast as well as teatime.

20

Clever cooks and minding manners

Here are some Georgian inventions that made life tastier.

1 Tasty toast The Georgians invented toast. A nasty Swedish visitor said the English invented toast because their houses were too chilly to spread butter on cold bread!

2 Yummy Yorkshires Ovens were improved so you could roast meat and cook a batter pudding in one at the same time. This pudding became known as a Yorkshire pudding. (Probably because it was eaten with roast Yorkshire terrier – only joking!) Yorkshire pudding was often a treat for Christmas Day.

3 Chocolate chunks Chocolate was drunk at the end of the 1600s – mixed with wine! The wine was heated and the chunk of chocolate grated into it. Sounds disgusting. Later, water was used to make hot chocolate and by the end of the 1700s you could eat chocolate bars.

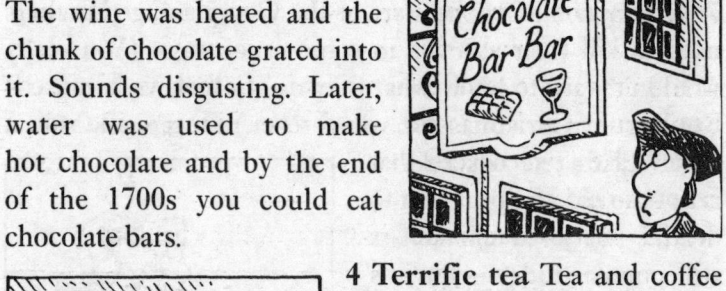

4 Terrific tea Tea and coffee were also popular with the rich in Georgian times. Tea was so expensive it was kept in a tea caddy with a lock on. There was a good trade in used tea-leaves. Traders put some colour back into the old tea leaves with chemicals. These chemicals could make you ill – or even kill you – but the traders didn't mind too much. (After all, they didn't drink the stuff!)

5 Spiffing spits Some cooks still roasted meat on a spit, but a Georgian spit could be turned by a clockwork motor. Poor people still roasted meat (when they could afford it) by hanging it by a hook from the mantelpiece over the fire. This was known as a 'danglespit' – no prizes for guessing why.

6 Super sandwiches In 1760 John Montague, the fourth Earl of Sandwich, was playing cards and didn't want to stop for dinner. He ordered that his meat be slapped between two pieces of bread so he could eat it while he played. Everyone started to copy him and asked for 'A beef as-eaten-by-John-Montague-the-fourth-Earl-of-Sandwich, please.' (The Romans had this idea more than 1,000 years before, but you don't eat a jam julius caesar, a ham hadrian or a peanut butter nero. You eat a *sandwich*.)

7 Kindly cooks At the start of the Georgian age butchers used to kill their animals in some cruel ways. (You really wouldn't want to know what they did to turkeys because it would ruin Christmas for you forever.) One recipe told a

cook, 'Take a red cockerel that is not too old and beat him to death.' (Battered chicken is still popular today – but it's not quite the same thing!) By the end of the Georgian period, you'll be pleased to hear, the killing of animals for food was kinder – but the animals still ended up just as dead.

8 Trendy teatime In the early 1700s people had dinner at two or three pm. By the end of the century this had moved to six or seven pm. Of course you'd get hungry long before that so fashionable people had 'afternoon tea' at about four o'clock. Did you realize that

your four o'clock tin of beans makes you a trendy Georgian?

9 Fab fruits The Georgians started to eat raw fruit. In earlier times doctors had said that eating fruit could spread

the plague! With new 'hot houses' the Georgians could grow their own exotic fruits, like grapes, peaches and pineapples. They also grew tomatoes and cooked them, but it was another 100 years before they ate them raw.

10 Cool rules Georgians wrote down rules on how the upper classes ought to behave at meal times. (You may like to try these at school dinners.)

• Guests walk in to the dining room in order, ladies first. Ladies and gentlemen sit next to one another. (At the start of the 1700s all the women had sat at one end and the men at the other.)

• Don't eat too quickly, because it shows you are too hungry.

• Don't eat too slowly, because that might mean you don't like your food.

- Never sniff your food when it's on the fork or the cook will think it's rotten.
- Don't scratch yourself, spit, blow your nose, lean your elbows on the table or sit too far back from the table.
- Do *not* pick your teeth before the plates are removed.
- If you need to go to the toilet then go and return quietly without telling everyone where you're going. (This was a great improvement on earlier dinner arrangements where pots were kept in the dining room for people to pee in!)

I PREFERRED THE OLD WAYS. YOU COULD CONTINUE TO CHAT WITH YOUR CHUMS AT THE TABLE AND TINKLE AT THE SAME TIME

Did you know ...?
Over in the American colonies in 1748 a schoolboy copied out rules from a French book of manners. He wrote, 'Do not clean your teeth with your fork, your knife or the tablecloth.' Clean your teeth with a tablecloth? Sadly the boy who wrote that mustn't have cleaned his teeth with *anything* because he ended up with false teeth made of wood. The boy's name was George Washington and he grew up to be America's first president.

Fatten up your friends
William Verral wrote a book called *The Cook's Paradise* with recipes for cooks to try. You can invite your friends to try this fairly simple recipe and it's pretty certain that it won't kill them. They may even enjoy it and invite you to share their next school dinner with you.

Strawberry fritters

You need:

450 g large strawberries (More if you have a lot of friends)

175 g plain flour

50 g caster sugar

2 teaspoons grated nutmeg

2 eggs

225 ml single cream

lard (you can use margarine though the Georgians hadn't invented it)

Method: Start this at least two hours before your guests arrive.

1 Dry the strawberries but leave the stalks on so you can hold them when you eat them.

2 Mix the flour, nutmeg and sugar in a bowl.

3 Beat the eggs, stir in the cream and slowly stir the mixture into the flour and sugar.

4 Leave this batter to stand for two hours.

5 Heat some lard in a frying pan. (It's best to get an adult to do this. If anyone's going to get burned it may as well be an adult rather than you. Adults are also useful for washing up your mess afterwards.)

6 Dip each strawberry in the batter – holding it by the stalk.

7 Drop a few strawberries into the hot lard and fry them gently till they are golden brown.

8 Drain them on kitchen towel and keep them warm in an oven while you cook the rest.

9 Eat the strawberries but not the stalks.

10 If you like them then share them with your friends. If you absolutely adore them then scoff the lot, describe the taste to your friends ... and tell them to cook their own.

Foul food

Not everything in the Georgian pantry was as tasty as strawberry fritters. There are a few gorgeous Georgian foods you may not like so much.

1 Daniel Defoe, the author of *Robinson Crusoe*, described his visit to Stilton, the town famous for its cheese …

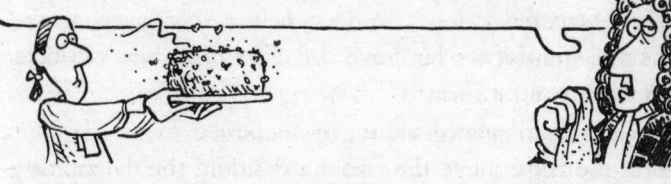

The cheese is brought to the table with the mites or maggots round it so thick that they bring a spoon with them to eat the mites with, as you do the cheese.

2 A doctor and writer, Tobias Smollett, complained about London bread …

The bread I eat in London is a harmful paste mixed with chalk and bone ashes, tasteless and bad for the health. The people know what is in it but prefer it to good corn bread because it is whiter.

IT'S TOTALLY POISONOUS BUT VERY WHITE

I'LL TAKE TWO

Smollett died when he was just 50. Maybe he ate too much bread!

3 Writer Jonathan Swift (famous for his book *Gulliver's Travels*) came up with a cure for the problem of food shortages in Ireland …

I have been told that a young, healthy child of a year old is a most delicious, nourishing and wholesome food, whether it's stewed, toasted, baked or boiled. I humbly suggest that 100,000 infants may be offered for sale to rich people in the kingdom. The mothers should try to make sure that they are plump and fat and good for the table.

I LOVE CHILDREN... BUT I COULDN'T EAT A WHOLE ONE

(He was joking, but making a serious point about how the Irish were treated.)

4 When a scientist took a close look at pepper he discovered that there was more in it than peppercorns. There was also the sweepings from the floors of the store-rooms. If there were mice and rats in the store-rooms then their droppings would be ground up with the pepper-powder. Of course, French shopkeepers ground in powdered dogs' droppings.

5 Milk was sold on the streets of cities by milk maids who carried it round the streets in open pails. The trouble was the pails collected extras on their journey. Tobias Smollett described them ...

Dirty water thrown from windows, spittle, snot and tobacco squirts from passersby, spatterings from coach wheels, dirt and trash chucked into it by roguish boys for the joke's sake, the spewings of infants and finally the lice that drop from the rags of the nasty drab woman that sells this precious mixture.

Top of the class

Daniel Defoe went on a tour of Britain and described the country. He thought Manchester was the 'greatest village in England' – so he'd be pleased to know the village football team is now doing well. He wrote that Liverpool was 'one of the wonders of Britain', and this was 200 years before The Beatles!

He also saw some pretty dreadful sights, especially among the poor people. The old ways were changing and, as usual, it meant the poor got poorer and the rich got richer. One of the problems was 'Enclosure.'

'What's that?' you cry! (Or if you *don't* cry it then your teacher probably will – and expect you to write about it in your next test.) So here's N. Idiot's guide to Enclosure …

HELLO! I AM N. IDIOT. NOW, YOU CAN CALL ME AN IDIOT IF YOU LIKE...BUT THINGS WERE BETTER IN THE GOOD OLD DAYS

The GOOD old DAYS before ENCLOSURE

Peasants share Common Land and Grow Crops.

Happy Peasant with his pig.

Happy Peasant's wife spins wool in happy cottage.

Unhappy Lord in Manor House wants that common land.

Happy pig and happy sheep.

Happy Peasant's happy children helping in the fields.

ENCLOSURE ACTS AFTER 1720 GOT RID OF THE OPEN FIELDS ALL OVER BRITAIN. MORE MONEY COULD BE MADE BY LESS PEOPLE
The BAD GEORGIAN days of ENCLOSURE
Fields fenced off so one Landowner can make more money.
Unhappy Peasant has to find work in town.
Unhappy Peasant's wife has to work in miserable mill.
TOWN
Happy Lord in Manor House owns the lot.
Unhappy Peasant children have to work in seedy slums, foul factories or murky mines.
Happy pig and sheep with flocks of friends.
ENCLOSURE MADE 'BRITAIN' RICHER ... AND MOST OF HER PEOPLE POORER. NOW, CALL ME AN IDIOT, BUT I WONDER IF IT WAS WORTH IT?

Daniel Defoe reckoned there were *seven* classes of people in Georgian Britain. Nothing is ever that simple, of course. But here are Defoe's seven classes. Which one would you like to have been in?

Class 7: 'The miserable, who really suffer want' In 1757 a mother and nine children in Buckinghamshire went several days without food. The mother found some money and bought the heart, liver and lungs of a calf to make a meal. Then she went off to gather fire wood. When she got back the children had eaten every scrap, gullet and all.

The same year a mother and two children in Cumberland had no bread and tried to survive on horse bran. They were all found dead one morning and the children had straw in their mouths.

Class 6: 'The poor, whose lives are hard' A family of seven in Derbyshire lived in a cave. The father was a lead miner and had been born in the cave, so had his five children. The cave was divided into three rooms by curtains and a hole had been dug through the roof to make a chimney. A pig and its piglets ran round the door. The miner earned about £6 a year and his wife could wash the lead ore and earn another £4 a year. Defoe wrote …

Things inside did not look as miserable as I'd expected. Everything was clean and neat and they seemed to live very pleasantly. The children looked plump and healthy, the woman was tall, clean and attractive.

When he gave her some money she almost fainted with happiness.

Class 5: 'The country people, who manage indifferently' (not too well) The days of the peasant families with their own strips of land were finished in Georgian times. A writer said the main problem was the country people owned nothing. Before Enclosure they used to keep a cow and a pony, a goose and a pig on the 'common' land. They'd have the odd wild rabbit, nuts and berries. But the common land was fenced off and sold to the richer farmers. The poor workers couldn't afford a large farm and there weren't any small ones. What was the point in working? A writer said …

> *Go to an ale house in the country and what will you find? It is full of men who could be working. They ask, 'If I work hard will I be allowed to build my own cottage? No. If I stay sober will I have land for a cow? No. If I save up can I get half an acre for potatoes? No. All you are offering me is the workhouse! Bring me another pot of ale.'*

Life in the country wasn't fresh air and roses. You worked when the farmer wanted you – harvest or sowing times – and you went hungry the rest of the year.

Class 4: 'The working trades, who labour hard but feel no want' The workers worked long hours, in terrible conditions, for poor pay. Yet in the north of England from the 1790s, tens of thousands flocked to the mills in the towns to get away from the country. They crowded into dark, filthy houses so they could be near their work. With children as young as five working, a family would have enough to eat and stay warm, but it wasn't much of a life.

Spinners worked 14 hours a day in steamy temperatures up to 90°C – it had to be steamy to stop the thread snapping.

The weavers were better paid and could earn £2 to £3 a week when Defoe was writing. But within a hundred years machines were replacing them and their wages fell to 12 shillings (60p) a week.

Builders built houses in the factory towns especially for weavers. They were built over ditches so the weavers could work in a nice damp cellar. It ruined their health but at least the threads didn't snap.

Class 3: 'The middle sort, who live well' The people in the middle didn't do too badly. Priests could be poor, but some had some very good parishes and lived very comfortably. A lady went to dinner with the Rector of Aston in 1779 and described her meal …

At three o'clock we sat down at table. It was covered at one end with a salmon in fennel sauce, melted butter, lemon pickle and soy; at the other end was a loin of veal roasted, on one side kidney beans, on the other side peas and in the middle a hot pigeon pie with yolk of egg in it. Next we were offered chicken and ham, then a currant tart followed by gooseberries, currants and melon, wines and cider.

Class 2: 'The rich, who live plentifully'

Some rich people thought the local village spoiled the view from their great houses ... so they knocked the village down and moved the poor somewhere else.

But other rich Georgians made their wealth by trading in people. Slavers. They captured Africans, transported them across the Atlantic Ocean like cattle and sold the ones who survived.

The slave journey wasn't the worst part of the experience. Being a slave was miserable. Nicholas Cresswell, a visitor to the West Indies in 1774, described their life ...

We went ashore and saw a cargo of slaves land. They were all naked except for a small piece of blue cloth. If they made the slightest mistake they were tied up and whipped without mercy. Some of them die under this harsh treatment.

Class 1: 'The great, who live profusely'

(with a lot to spare) Most lords managed to earn £5,000 a year – that's about £300,000 today. They enjoyed their money. Some of the great country houses you can see today were built in the Georgian period. In 1762 George III bought 'The Queen's House' in London

and turned it into Buckingham Palace. (It cost him £21,000 – the price a dog would pay for a kennel in London today.)

The Duke of Chandos had his own orchestra of 27 musicians while Sir Robert Walpole spent £1,500 a year on wine (£90,000 today) and £1 every night on candles, (the miserable could buy food, drink, fuel and shelter for five weeks for that £1).

BUT ... the 'great' needed the votes of the lower classes when it came to elections for parliament. They had to invite the farmers into their great homes! Yeuch! The Earl of Cork whinged ...

> *At election time I have to open my doors to every dirty fellow in the county who has a vote. All my best floors are spoiled by the hobnailed boots of the farmers stamping about them. Every room is a pigsty and the Chinese wallpaper in the drawing room stinks so terrible of tobacco that it would knock you down to walk into it.*

Poor Earl of Cork!

Posh politics

The posh Georgians in Britain sent people to 'Parliament' to argue with the king. Where did this Parliament thing come from? Here's a quick horrible history ...

♔ The first big argument was in 1215 when the posh people of England (the Barons) fell out with King John. They made him sign a great charter (posh name: Magna Carta). This said he couldn't have everything his own way just because he was king. John sulked but he signed.

♔ Then along came King Henry III who forgot all about the Magna Carta and started demanding money. So one of the Barons, Simon de Montfort, organized a group of Barons to talk about horrible Henry. They talked in French ('cos they was posh). French for 'to talk' is parler so a talk-shop is 'parler-ment' or Parliament. Geddit?

♔ Simple Simon went to war with Henry. He lost at the Battle of Evesham and had his head cut off – not to mention his arms and his legs! But his Parliament idea lived on.

♔ Members of Parliament (MPs for short) were the chief men of the towns and counties. The rich men voted for them and sent them to argue with the kings and queens. (Women, even rich, posh women, had no say at all.) Sometimes the MPs got really angry and turned nasty – in 1647 they went to war with King Charles I and ended up cutting his head off.

♔ The last Stuart Queen, Anne, enjoyed going to Parliament and listening to them talk. But she didn't argue with them very much. The situation was desperate! Who on earth could they argue with? They began to argue with each other, and split up into two parties – one lot were nicknamed the 'Whigs' and the other lot were called the 'Tories'. These were actually very insulting names. A 'Whig' was a Scottish robber who usually murdered his victim, while a 'Tory' was an Irish cattle thief. The queen cheated a bit to make sure her favourites, the Tories, stayed in power.

That brings us to the gorgeous Georgians …

Potty parties

Disaster! King George I didn't do a lot of arguing with his Parliament because he hardly spoke any English. He gave a lot of presents and power to the Whigs and they ruled the country for him. The Tories hated George I – they only supported him because they thought he was better than the Catholic James Stuart. Even the Whigs didn't like him much!

Parliament now had the power!

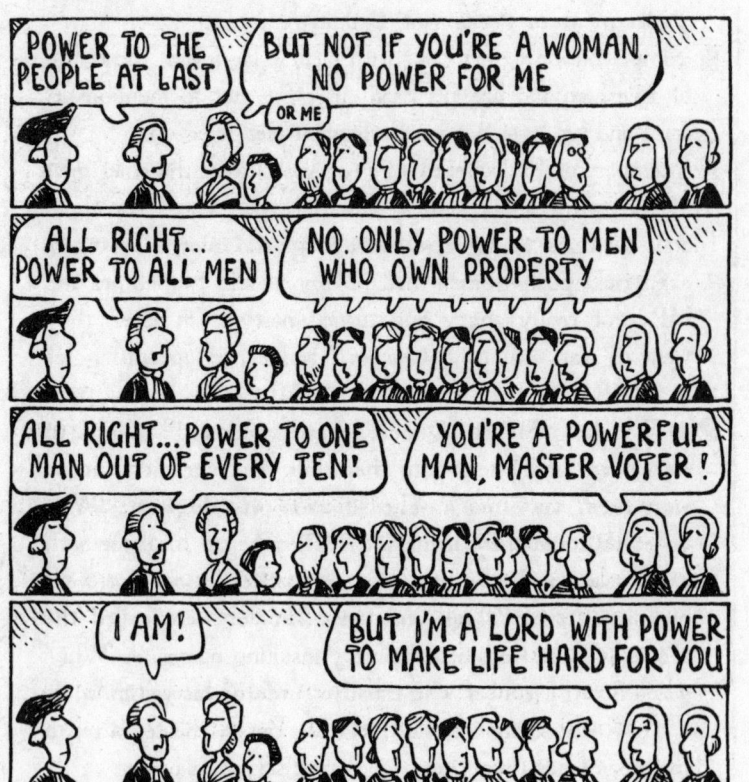

There were more Lords' sons in the House of Commons than any other group.

Did you know …?
- Some places had so few voters they could be paid to vote the way someone wanted – they were called 'rotten boroughs'.
- Some of the growing factory towns couldn't send anyone to Parliament at all.
- Some places were run by a powerful family who could send anyone to Parliament they liked – these were known as 'pocket boroughs'.
- MPs weren't paid. Only rich men could afford to be MPs. Who would they stick up for in Parliament? Their rich friends, of course.

The way Britain picked its politicians was unfair and potty. No wonder the Georgians got so many ...

Peculiar prime ministers

Wily Walpole

One man whose family ran a pocket borough was Sir Robert Walpole. He is the man that historians call the first prime minister – King George I's top dog in the House of Commons.

But the title prime minister was an insult! It meant 'King George's favourite creep in parliament'. (It's a bit like someone calling you a teacher's pet!) So Robert Walpole said, 'I am NOT a prime minister.' Then he went on not being a prime minister for the next 21 years. (That's still the record, Mr Blair! Can you beat it?)

He had a good way to make sure he won every vote in parliament. He paid the MPs to vote the way he wanted.

EVERY MAN HAS HIS PRICE

This is dishonest – Britain got the laws that the rich paid for, not the laws that the poor needed – but no one seemed to mind too much.

Poorly Pitt

William Pitt (the Elder) – PM in 1757 – was dead honest. He did not believe in bribing MPs, unlike Walpole. But he did find the job a strain. He became almost mad with the strain and the cure was to lock him in a darkened room. His wife passed food through to him.

Being half mad didn't stop George III being king and it didn't stop Pitt being prime minister. They let him out of the room to speak in the House of Lords. This was a big mistake. While he was speaking he collapsed and died.

No-good North

Lord North – PM in 1770 – has been called the worst prime minister ever. He soon got bored in Parliament and would nod off to sleep. He'd ask to be woken up when the speaker got to the end. He was also the ugliest prime minister Britain has ever had.

Lord North often complained that it was a terrible strain being prime minister …

> *I'd rather be hanged than suffer the pain of running the king's business.*

So, how did he get the job? When he was a boy he was a playmate of King George III, so George gave him the PM job.

Portable Pitt
William Pitt (the Younger) – PM from 1783 – was honest like his dear departed Dad. And, like his Dad, was pretty miserable in his job. He was the youngest prime minister ever at the age of 24.

He led Britain through many of its years of war with France. He made the proud boast …

> *I can save this country, and no one else can.*

He did this by raising new taxes. He put a tax on houses with more than seven windows – some grumpy Georgians just bricked up the extra windows to dodge the tax! But as he lay ill in 1806 he heard that Napoleon had battered the Brit armies at Austerlitz and he groaned …

> *Oh, my country. How I leave my country!*

The man who'd boasted, 'I can save my country' did the most sensible thing possible. He died straight after saying those words.

He broke another record: he became the youngest prime minister ever to *die* in office when he popped his parliamentary clogs at the age of 46. It wasn't the darkened room that killed this Pitt but the bottles of port wine he swilled.

Potted Perceval
Spencer Perceval – PM in 1812 – was about as popular as the plague. A man called Bellingham was imprisoned in Russia and lost all his money. Bellingham thought the British government should give him back the money he'd lost. The government said, 'No'. Bellingham said, 'Right! I'll show you!' and he took a pistol into the House of  Commons where he shot PM Perceval dead. He's the only British PM ever to be assassinated.

Crowds came out onto the street to cheer, 'Perceval is dead! Hurrah!'

Pretty soon Bellingham was dead too because he was hanged. (This was cheaper than paying him the money he wanted.)

Prime ministers have their famous last words recorded by historians for teachers to bore you with. At least PM Perceval left us with a nice short final speech:

OUCH!

Cheerless for children

One of the worst classes to be in was the 'children's' class.

Children were dressed as adults and often worked as adults from a very early age. The hard part was surviving childhood ...

1 First you had to survive being born. One child out of three didn't live to be 15, and careless mothers cost babies' lives. There were many cases of a baby sharing a bed with mother, father, brothers or sisters and being smothered when someone rolled on top of them in their sleep.

2 Poor families could not afford too many children. There were cases of babies being left in the streets to die, or strangled and dumped on the local rubbish tip or into a drain.

3 Next you had to survive your christening. At a christening in Surrey a nurse got very drunk. She undressed the baby and went to put it in its cradle. By mistake she put it too close to a large fire which killed it in a few minutes. She told the judges who tried her that she thought the baby was a log of firewood. The judges set her free! (Georgian judges were often drunk in court. The nurse's judges must have been if they thought a baby and a log could be mistaken!

They probably said, 'She was so drunk she wooden know the difference.')

4 A child who was brought up by a paid child-minder, a 'nurse', was unlucky. Children with nurses were twice as likely to die. Nurses were well known for being drunk. Nurses of poor children often deliberately damaged the child's face or legs so the child would grow up to be a more pitiful sight. The nurse would then hire out the child to a beggar who would make more money.

5 Thomas Coram opened a hospital for unwanted children in 1741. He was flooded with so many sick and dying babies, dumped on the doorstep, that about 10,000 of the children died. But his good example led the later Georgians to look after poor children better.

6 Young girls in rich homes had to grow up to be ladies with fine figures. That meant having a narrow waist. Some were fitted with a steel cage under their clothes that pinched their stomachs in. The pinching went a little too far with Elizabeth Evelyn. She died. Elizabeth was *two* years old!

SUCH A FASHIONABLE SHAPE FOR HER FIGURE

AND A FASHIONABLE SHADE OF BLUE FOR HER FACE

7 Orphans could have a terribly tough time. To keep large numbers of them quiet at night they'd be given a mixture called Godfrey's cordial which was full of the powerful drug opium. It sent them to sleep all right – but give them too much and they didn't wake up ... ever!

8 Children were often taken from orphanages to become servants. But Elizabeth Brownrigg treated them more like slaves. Girls were kept in filthy cellars, left in the cold with no clothes and constantly whipped. They slept on rotten straw and were given scraps to eat. Of course many girls died after this sort of treatment. Then one escaped and reported Elizabeth Brownrigg to the parish officers. They visited the Brownrigg house and found another girl on the point of death. They arrested Brownrigg and she was hanged.

9 Then you had to survive school. Some poor children went to 'dame' schools run by a local woman or to 'charity' schools, paid for by rich people in the area. But 'public' schools, where rich parents paid to send their children, were in a dreadful state in Georgian times. Teachers were violent and pupils were worse! A boy wrote home to complain about his life in the bedrooms: 'I have been woken up many times by the hot points of cigars burning holes in my face.'

MORNING, SMITHERS

10 But children *did* fight back! In 1793 there was a 'Great Rebellion' at Winchester school. The boys took over a tower at the school and refused to come down. The gentle boys threw stones at the teachers below – the not-so-gentle ones fired pistols! At the same school in 1818 a pupil rebellion had to be dealt with by soldiers using bayonets.

NAPOLEON'S CAVALRY IS ONE THING, BUT ARMED ANGRY PUBLIC SCHOOLBOYS ARE QUITE ANOTHER

BANG POP

Did you know …?
One of Winchester's old pupils, Thomas Arnold, went as head teacher to Rugby School and wrote the famous book *Tom Brown's School Days* about life there. But Rugby had its own problems before Arnold got the job there. In 1797 a gang of pupils used gunpowder to blow up the headmaster's door! (And you thought you were daring when you dropped a stink-bomb in school assembly?)

Wild women

Being a child wasn't fun – but it was probably worse being a woman. Men expected their wives to be quiet and to obey them. But there were times when a bit of wildness in a woman came in handy.

In Georgian times it was women who went to market to buy the corn. If the price of corn was too high then their families would go hungry. And it was the women who bullied the farmers into cutting their prices.

The wild women of Bewdley, for example, cut open sacks of wheat and told the farmers they would only pay what people were paying in nearby towns. The women won.

In Exeter, the townsmen heard that farmers were going to put up the prices of corn. They sent their women to market to argue for a lower price ... or 'take it by force'! The women won again.

In Bewdley and Exeter the men were happy to stand back and send the women to battle for the food.

Of course, women were not treated so well when it came to work and pay ... especially pay. Women worked as hard as men in the farmers' fields – but they were paid half as much. Then, when farm jobs were short, it was the women who got the sack.

But what was it like for Georgian women? Test your brainpower with this simple test. Which of these foul facts were true for woeful Georgian women?

1 Georgian men believed that women were not as intelligent as they were.

2 Georgian girls married when they were just 12 years old.

3 A woman who killed her husband could be burned alive as a punishment.

4 Some men would get rid of a wife by selling her at an auction.

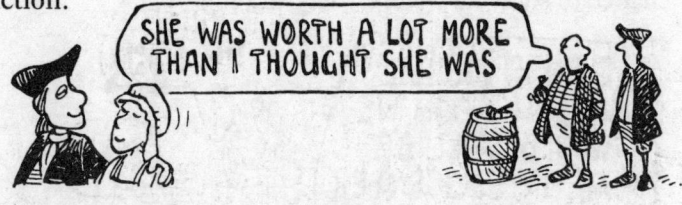

5 A husband who beat his wife would be punished.

6 Women used arsenic poison to make themselves look beautiful.

7 In the middle of the 1700s a hard-working man in industry could earn £3 a week – a maidservant in a house would earn £3 *a year*!

8 Lady Wortley Montague was famous for being the cleanest woman in Britain.

9 A woman could be divorced if she'd used make-up to trick a man into marrying her.

10 Fashionable women wore masks to keep the sun off their faces.

Answers:

1 True. That's what they believed. Of course they were wrong. Women were every bit as intelligent as men but were not given a good education and didn't have the chance to show how clever they were.

EVEN IF YOU HAD AN EDUCATION, WE WOULD STILL BE MORE INTELLIGENTER

2 False. The average age was about 24. Very few married at under 16 but there is a curious report of a Christchurch parson who married a girl of 13. He was 83 years old at the time. But he was seriously weird. He was a rich man who dressed so carelessly he was often mistaken for a tramp.

3 True. A man murdering his wife was hanged but women could be burned. In 1726, Catherine Hayes was sentenced to die at the stake. The 'kind' judges decided she would be strangled first so she didn't suffer death by burning. But the flames were lit too soon and the executioner couldn't reach her to kill her quickly. In Maidstone in 1769 Susannah Lott died at the stake before she was burned and didn't suffer so much. This law was finally changed in 1789 so women got equal rights – the right to be hanged for murder.

4 True. It was not legal but it sometimes happened. The woman was taken to market with a rope round her neck and sold to the highest bidder. Sometimes a woman would fetch a few pounds and sometimes she could be traded for an ox – better for pulling a plough, of course, but it didn't make such a good cup of tea. This uncommon sort of divorce was last heard of in 1887.

5 False. A husband was allowed to beat his wife. The stick he used must be no thicker than his thumb, so he could whip her with a cane but probably not a walking stick.

6 True. The white powder was put on the skin to make it pale and smooth and beautiful. If too much of the white poison got into your mouth you'd be pale and smooth and dead. This happened to a famous beauty, Maria Gunning in the 1750s. (She was warned!) There was also poisonous mercury and lead in some of this make-up which could make you go bald. And it was a mistake to kiss these women! There was a scandal in Italy when over 600 men died from getting too close to wives wearing arsenic make-up!

7 True. A mirror in a great house like Holkham Hall, Norfolk, was said to have cost £500. If a £3-a-year maid broke that mirror then the owners would have to stop her wages for 166 years and eight months to pay for it.

8 False. Lady Wortley Montague was filthy. She was once told that her hands were rather dirty. She replied, 'If you think they are dirty then you ought to see my feet!'

9 True. In 1770 the British government passed a law saying a woman who tricked a man with make-up was as bad as a witch. If he married her, and found she was ugly underneath all the powder and paint, then he could be un-married any time he wanted.

10 True. A pale skin was beautiful to the Georgians. A mask in front of the face would protect the skin. Of course it was awkward trying to hold a mask up so some had a button attached to the back and the button was held between the teeth. These masks had eye cut-outs so were suntanned eyeballs all right?

Gruesome Georgians

Georgian Britain was a prime crime time. In 1700 there were about 50 crimes that could be punished by death. By 1822 they had lost count! There were at least 200 hanging crimes and some experts believe there were as many as 350! These included ...

- Going armed in disguise (so the Lone Ranger would have been in trouble)
- Poaching fish (but a poached egg was fine)
- Forging bank notes (but not sick notes to teachers, so you'd have been safe)1
- Cutting down trees (with criminals rooted out by the men of Special Branch).

And, of course, murder ...

The mystery of the moors

Daniel Clarke was a Yorkshire shoemaker who married a wealthy woman. The trouble was he liked to boast about his riches. 'I'm the richest man in Knaresborough! You should see my jewels!'

On 8 February 1745 he disappeared, never to be seen alive again.

Law officers found some of Clarke's jewels in the house of a man called Eugene Aram. Aram was arrested but said Clarke had given them to him before he left the county. The magistrates had to let Eugene Aram go free.

Of course, as you may have guessed, Aram had murdered Clarke and stolen the jewels. Not only did he get away with it, but he got to keep the jewels and he moved to Kings Lynn in Norfolk. He had got away with murder! Until ...

1. In 1820, 46 people were hanged for forging banknotes. But after the executions, some of the notes were shown to be genuine. Oops!

Fourteen years later a labourer was digging for limestone in a cave when he came across some human bones. No one could prove that they were the bones of Daniel Clarke, but Eugene Aram was arrested anyway. He was found guilty and hanged. His body was hung in a cage by the Knaresborough road where the murder happened. As the body rotted, and the bones fell through the bars of the cage, his widow was allowed to pick them up. But one night a doctor took the skull and it's still on view in the Royal College of Surgeons' Museum in London.

Gruesome!

So here's the mystery. What sort of man would murder the shoemaker for his money? Can you guess? Was Eugene Aram …

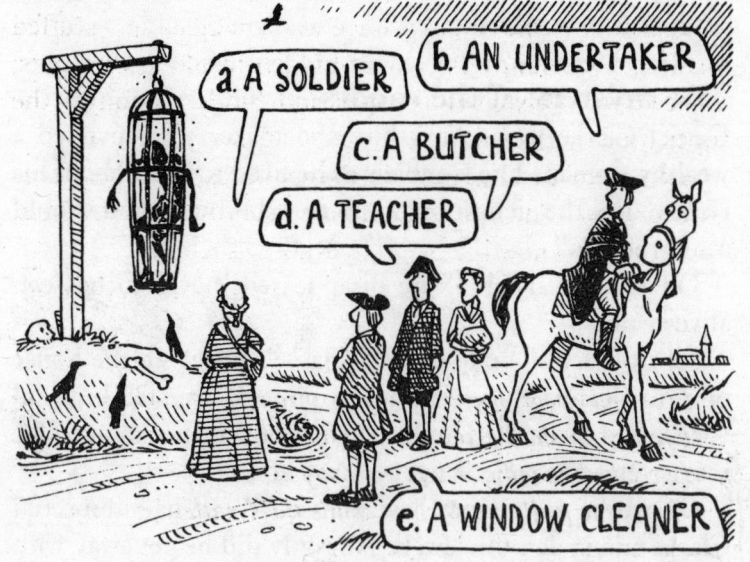

a. A SOLDIER
b. AN UNDERTAKER
c. A BUTCHER
d. A TEACHER
e. A WINDOW CLEANER

Answer: d) Eugene Aram was an English teacher. Which just goes to show … something!

Heroes and villains

The Georgians had some pretty famous villains. The trouble is they became heroes, a bit like Robin Hood. You know the sort of thing ...

I ONLY ROB THE RICH

'COS THE POOR HAVE NOTHING WORTH PINCHING!

Take smugglers, for example. Georgian Britain was a time for smuggling. Lots of people seemed to think they were doing a good job – half the tea drunk in Britain was smuggled in to the country. Lace was smuggled in – stuffed inside geese; brandy kegs were hidden inside lobster pots; tobacco was twisted into ropes and hidden amongst the ropes used on the ships.

All good fun and part of the game called 'cheat-the-government'. Smugglers today are seen as brave outlaws. You probably know the poem by Rudyard Kipling ...

Five and twenty ponies, trotting through the dark –
Brandy for the Parson, baccy for the Clerk;
Laces for the lady, letters for a spy,
Watch the wall, my darling, while the Gentlemen go by.

The trouble was these 'gentlemen' were nasty, cruel and greedy. They'd probably cut your throat just for the fun of it and then say, 'You still think I'm a hero?'

In 1748 a man called Chater betrayed a smuggling gang and a law officer called Galley tried to arrest them. A magazine of the time described what happened next …

They began with poor Galley, cut off his nose, broke every joint of him and after several hours of torture dispatched him. Chater they carried to a dry well, hung him by the middle to a cross beam in it, leaving him to perish with hunger and pain. But when they came, several days after, and heard him groan, they cut the rope, let him drop to the bottom and threw in logs and stones to cover him. The person who told the magistrates the story was in disguise because he feared the same would happen to him.

Some 'gentlemen' they turned out to be.

Never mind the story books and poems. Here is the terrible truth about these exciting criminals!

The highwayman
Name: Dick Turpin (also called himself John Palmer)
Claim to fame: Highwayman
Life: 1705 – 1739
The story:
- Brave and handsome hero who was a wonderful rider.
- He robbed stage coaches but was always very polite … especially to ladies.
- He rode his gallant horse, Black Bess, all the way from

Essex to York in record time to prove he couldn't have committed a crime … though he had.

The terrible truth:

- He was a butcher boy till he decided there was more money in stealing cattle than chopping them. He joined 'The Essex Gang' of violent house-breakers. They entered someone's home, robbed it and tortured the occupants till they handed over their money and valuables.

- When most of the Gang was arrested Turpin tried his hand at a different crime. He stopped a gentleman on the road and threatened him with a pistol. That man was Tom King, the famous highwayman. King took Turpin as a partner. They spent two years terrorizing the Essex roads. When King was caught Turpin tried to rescue him but accidentally shot his partner dead!

- Turpin was arrested for stealing sheep in Yorkshire. No one knew he was the famous highwayman until his old teacher recognized his handwriting! Turpin ended up hanged in York. He never made the famous ride on Black Bess – though another highwayman, John Nevison, may have done.

Not to be confused with: Black Beauty, Turnip Townsend, Mashed Turnip.

The outlaw

Name: Rob Roy MacGregor (also known as Red Roy or Robert the Red. When he joined the English he changed his name to Robert Campbell.)

Claim to fame: Outlaw

Life: 1671 – 1734

The story:

- Poor Rob was the Scottish Robin Hood. He was outlawed just because he was from the clan MacGregor, not because he was a criminal. For years he lived in caves and woods, often escaping the law by the skin of his teeth.

- He led his poor neighbours in their struggle against cattle thieves from the north. Rob Roy led them to freedom from the terror.

- He fought bravely for his country in their struggle against the English.

The terrible truth:

- A cattle thief by the age of 20. He fought for Scotland in the Glorious Revolution against England – but switched sides when he saw he was going to lose.

- Became a respectable cattle dealer but, when times got hard, he took his customers' money and ran off with it to the Western Isles.

- While he lived as a bandit he threatened cattle owners: 'Pay me to leave your cattle alone.' Switched sides again and fought against the English but was captured. King George pardoned him. He went home to live a quiet life.

Not to be confused with: Red Rum, Roy of the Rovers.

The pirate
Name: Blackbeard (full name Edward Teach, also known as Tache or Thatch – though he was christened Edward Drummond)
Claim to fame: Pirate
Life: Born in Bristol, date unknown, died 1718

The story:

• Blackbeard went into battle with six pistols at his waist and lighted matches under his hat to make him look frightening. (He was a bit of a hot-head.)

• He was a brave English hero who stole from the French. His treasure was buried on a desert island and no one has found it to this day.

• Blackbeard died fighting against a small army. When his body was thrown into the sea it swam round the ship three times before it sank.

The terrible truth:

• Blackbeard was a vicious bully. He went into business with the Governor of North Carolina in America. The Governor let Blackbeard attack ships – any ships, not just the French – so long as he got a share of the loot.

• The 'treasure' wasn't gold and jewels but goods like barrels of sugar. The American people (not the French) became so fed up with Blackbeard they sent a naval ship to stop him.

• In a hand-to-hand battle Lieutenant Robert Maynard shot Blackbeard dead – then cut his head off just to make sure.

Not to be confused with: Bluebeard, King Edward potatoes, teachers called Edward, Margaret Thatcher, Black Bess, Black Beauty, black pudding – and there's no truth in the story that his crew said a Teach should be nicknamed Blackboard!

And, talking about pirates …

Pirates, parrots and eye-patches

Have you ever seen a film about pirates? They were funny old characters, and liked a good laugh and a quick chorus of 'Fifteen men on a dead man's chest, yo-ho-ho and a bottle of rum!' Then they battled bravely against huge Spanish galleons and made the cowardly captains cough up some terrific treasure.

Right?

Wrong.

Here is the terrible truth about the gorgeous Georgian pirates:

1 Spanish treasure ships By Georgian times there were no Francis Drake characters attacking Spanish galleons and winning gold for England and the Queen. They attacked little trading ships to steal tobacco or slaves or just spare sails and anchor cable. ('Your anchor cable or your life?' doesn't sound so gorgeous, does it?)

2 Head-scarves Did they really tie large, coloured handkerchiefs round their heads? Yes. (If you want to try this then use a clean hankie. 'Snot very nice otherwise.)

3 Walking the plank Have you ever seen the play *Peter Pan*? Cut-throat Captain Hook plans to make the Lost Boys walk the plank and drop off into crocodile-infested waters. Very dramatic. But true? No. Pirates couldn't be bothered with that sort of play-acting. Some cruel pirates did tell their captives, 'You're free to walk home!' while they were in the middle of shark-filled seas. If they wanted to get rid of their victims then they just hacked them to death and threw them over the side. (That's a bit boring – especially for the victim, who'd be bored to death – but it saved a lot of time.)

4 Marooning Did they really leave a sailor on some desert island with a bottle of water and a gun? Yes, they did. It was a punishment usually kept for pirates who tried to desert their shipmates. The most famous marooned sailor was Alexander Selkirk whose adventures were turned into the story *Robinson Crusoe*. (Imagine being alone and lonely with no friendly human to talk to. You'd go mad. And teachers are still doing this today. They call it detention.)

5 The Jolly Roger flag Did pirates fly the black flag with a white skull and crossbones? Sometimes. Most Tudor and Stuart pirates flew a red flag – they put a story around that the flag was dyed with blood. Georgian pirates started to come up with their own designs. (What picture would you have on your flag to strike terror into the hearts of your enemies? A school and cross boys, perhaps.)

HOW DO YOU SUPPOSE THAT IS GOING TO STRIKE TERROR INTO THE HEARTS OF OUR ENEMIES?

6 Wooden legs Did pirates limp around on wooden legs? Some did. Fighting against the cannon of naval vessels was dangerous, and legs, arms and heads must have flown around like skittles in a bowling alley. Of course they didn't have doctors on board to make a neat job of a mangled arm or leg – but the ship's carpenter could carve you a neat replacement.

7 Parrots Did pirates have parrots on their shoulders? Not usually – but they often carried them in cages back to Britain from South America. They could teach them to speak during the voyage back across the Atlantic then sell them as pets in Britain.

8 Buried treasure Much more money has been spent *searching* for pirate treasure than has ever been *found*. If you won a million on the lottery would you bury it? No, you'd want to spend it. So did the pirates. Was there ever such a place as Treasure Island? The writer Robert Louis Stevenson spent a wet holiday in Scotland in 1881 and painted a map of an island for fun. He named it Skeleton Island and liked it so much he wrote the book *Treasure Island* to go with the map. Stevenson never met a pirate and he pinched the 'Dead man's chest' song from another writer's book.

VISITORS!

WHAT D'YER THINK IS IN THE CHEST?

LUNGS?

9 Keel hauling A pirate found guilty of a crime against the crew would be forced to swallow cockroaches – if he was lucky! If he was unlucky he'd be *keel hauled*. A rope was tied under his arms and another to his feet. He was thrown into the sea and dragged under the bottom of the boat ('hauled' under the 'keel'). He might survive drowning but there were very rough barnacles clinging to the bottom of a wooden ship that would scrape the skin. (And, when he got back, the rotten crew didn't even give him an Elastoplast!)

10 Gold earrings Did tough pirates wear pretty gold rings in their ears? Yes! They were a superstitious lot and believed that a gold earring gave them better eye sight. (A pirate never wore glasses, because he didn't want to make a spectacle of himself.)

Painful punishments

Georgians tried to be tough on criminals. Hangings were performed in public so everyone could see what happened to naughty boys and girls.

Of course the Georgian newspapers loved crime stories as much as today's papers. Here are some genuine press cuttings ...

Fortune-telling

A local record book records a curious crime and a cruel punishment in the north of England ...

Susannah Fleming stood in the pillory at White Cross for an hour for fortune-telling. Though she was not bothered by the public she was nearly strangled either because she fainted or because her neck was held too tightly. A sailor, out of kindness, brought her down the ladder on his back in nearly a dying state.

Suicide

The Georgians thought they were wiser than the people of the Middle Ages and Tudor times. But old superstitions lingered on.

Killing yourself was against the law, so it had to be punished. How do you punish people who have killed themselves? The Georgians had no problem. *The Western Flying Post* newspaper reported the death of an old man in 1755 ...

On 6 June an old man hanged himself by his handkerchief at Linkincehorn in Cornwall. The coroner decided that he had committed suicide. He was buried at Kesbrook Crossroad and a stake driven through his body.

A suicide victim could not be buried in a churchyard because, the Georgians said, he had gone against God's law. He was buried at the crossroads so the ghost would be confused about which way to go to get back home. Why a stake through his body? Because people believed this would stop the man rising from his grave and haunting the area.

STAKE NOT STEAK!

Sheep-stealing
Stealing a sheep could be punished by hanging in Georgian times – a 12 year-old boy was sentenced to death for stealing a lamb in 1802. But one sheep thief saved the law officers a rope! He stole a sheep and managed to hang himself. In 1762 the *Gloucester Journal* reported …

On Tuesday afternoon a man was found strangled in a field. He had stolen a sheep and, to carry it away, had tied the back legs and put the cord over his head. When he rested on a gate the sheep kicked, the cord dropped over his neck and strangled him.

At least he died with a *sheepish* grin on his face. The good news is the sheep lived. The bad news is it was certainly eaten by someone else not long after.

Did you know …?
Prison in Georgian times was not like prison today. Prisoners could keep pets. But in 1714, Newgate Prison in London banned one of the most popular pets: pigs.

WE'RE TREATED LIKE ANIMALS IN HERE!

Witchcraft

The ancient way of testing for witchcraft was to throw a suspect into water and see if they floated – a witch would float (be taken out, hanged and die) while an innocent person would sink (probably drown and die anyway).

Ruth Osborne was beaten and drowned at Tring in 1751 as a suspected witch. Twenty years later, in the same town, a man and his wife both suffered the 'water ordeal' – the woman died and the man *just* survived.

But things were changing. In 1770 a man accused a 55-year-old woman of witchcraft. She said, 'I don't think I'm a witch – but you'd better try me, just to make sure!' The *Northampton Mercury* newspaper described what happened …

A miller in the area was chosen to perform the ducking ceremony. The poor woman went to the mill where a great number of people were gathered. The miller remembered what had happened in Tring and refused to try her in front of such a large crowd. He promised he would try her, in secret, as soon as he was alone.

The crowd left. The woman survived. We can guess that the miller didn't try too hard to drown her. Wise man. Maybe the Georgians were learning some common sense after all.

Theft

Any sort of theft was punished very harshly in Georgian times. In Norwich a girl was hanged for stealing a petticoat. No one seemed to object, though the girl was just seven years old.

Bodies for sale

Wild life, wilder death

Jonathan Wild was a thief-taker. He promised to find your stolen goods for you … if you paid him a reward, of course.

People came to him from all over London. 'Can you get back my stolen property?' they asked.

'I'll leave messages in certain places,' he said. 'The thieves will leave your stolen goods where I can find them. I will leave them a reward. Everybody's happy.'

'You are wonderful, Mr Wild.'

'I know,' he said.

The truth was that Jonathan Wild had organized the robbery in the first place! No wonder he knew how to get the stolen property back. In time every thief in London was working for Wild and every victim in London came to him for help.

No thief dared to upset Wild because Wild would simply betray the thief to the law. He had 75 criminals convicted and 60 of those were hanged.

Wild grew rich and fat. By 1724 he was in complete control of London crime. But in the end Wild's wickedness was uncovered and he was hanged. Thousands gathered to pelt him with mud and stones as he was taken to the gallows.

Yet Wild still had some friends left and they did a curious thing. They smuggled his dead body away and buried it in a secret place at the dead of night. Why would they do such a thing? Because they were afraid William Cheselden would get his hands on the body. Mr Cheselden was a surgeon and he was interested in learning about the human body by cutting up dead ones. (He was also interested in cutting up live ones but they wouldn't let him!)

Where did Mr Cheselden get his dead bodies from? He

bought bodies of criminals who'd been hanged. That's what Wild's friends were afraid of.

Did Cheselden get Wild's body? Yes. The secret grave was found, the body was dug up and delivered to the surgeon. (The skeleton of Wild can still be seen today in the Hunterian Museum at the Royal College of Surgeons if you are sick-minded enough to want to look at it.)

The age of the bodysnatcher had begun!

'Better get back in your coffin, mate!' – a gorgeous Georgian tale of terror
Edward Henson was crying and the tears spilled into his ale. 'You're pathetic,' the landlord said. 'You're drunk.'

'I'm not,' Edward argued but his voice was slurred and his eyes were rolling in his leather-skinned face.

'I've seen a lot of drunks in my time and I tell you, sailor, you're drunk. You don't even know that you're crying into your beer,' the landlord sneered, wiping a greasy hand on his stained apron.

The air of the quayside tavern was smoky with

the cheap tallow candles and shadows hid the filth on the floor. 'I'm sad,' Edward moaned.

'You'll get no more ale in this tavern,' the landlord said firmly.

'No! Listen. I had a friend. The best friend a man ever had. His name was Geordie. Poor Geordie.'

Edward took a deep drink of the clouded drink and wiped his mouth on the back of his sleeve, then he wiped his nose, then he wiped his eyes. 'He's dead.'

'I'm sorry,' the landlord said. 'What did he die of?'

'Don't know. I'm not a doctor. He woke up yesterday morning and he was dead!' the sailor said.

'These things happen,' the landlord shrugged.

'I went to Geordie's funeral this afternoon. Sort of said goodbye to him. We've sailed together for ten years or more. All over the world.'

The landlord slipped onto the bench alongside the drunken sailor and lowered his voice. 'I hope he rests in peace,' he said.

'He will, he will. He'll go straight to heaven, will Geordie.'

'I'm sure his soul will go to heaven,' the landlord said. 'It's his body I'd worry about.'

'His body? It's dead. I saw it myself! I said, "You're quiet this morning Geordie," and he never replied. That's because he was dead, you know. Did I tell you he was dead?'

The landlord grabbed the sailor's arm and shook him. 'The sack-'em-up men are in this town.'

'Shack-'em who?'

'Sack-'em-up men! Bodysnatchers! In the past six weeks we've lost five bodies from the local churchyard.'

'Lost them? How can you lose a body?'

'They were dug up, put in a sack and taken to the hospital.'

'So the doctors could make them better?' Edward said cheerfully. 'Will they make my friend Geordie better?'

'No! The doctors want to cut them up. To try their experiments on. If you don't want your friend to end up on a doctor's table then you'd better go and have a look at the grave tonight. But be careful. These sack-'em-up men aren't too fussy about what they take. If they catch you interfering they'll slap a pitch plaster over your mouth to shut you up.'

'A pitch plaster? I'll suffocate!' the sailor cried.

'Then that'll save them digging up your friend,' the landlord warned. 'Most people watch their friends' graves in groups of four or five. Some people even sleep near the graves for two or three weeks.'

'Two or three weeks?'

'Till the body's too rotten to be any use to the doctors,' the landlord explained.

'My ship sails in two days,' Edward moaned.

'But tonight's the night when the sack-'em-up men will be after him.' The landlord took the sailor's ale tankard and helped him to his feet. Out of the door, turn right and climb

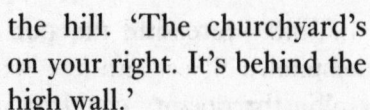

the hill. 'The churchyard's on your right. It's behind the high wall.'

Edward Henson looked almost sober as he said, 'Thank you. I'll go and look after Geordie.'

He staggered towards the door, crashing against tables and upsetting tankards. The night air was damp and there was a light, chill mist blurring the moon. Edward took a few deep breaths and used the wall to guide himself along the muddy lane that ran along the river front.

The mist seemed to deaden the sounds of the night. All the sailor could hear was the squish of his boots in the mud and his own creaking breathing. The pie stall at the end of Low Row was closed. Two men had been there earlier in the night with their cheerful cries of 'Chelsea buns!', 'Pies all smoking hot!' and 'Mutton pies!' Edward suddenly realized that he was hungry. He turned away from the deserted pie stall and up the hill. He passed the small stone prison cell at the foot of Crown Street and left behind the pitiful sobbing of its solitary prisoner.

After ten minutes he reached a high wall that was soft and slimy to the touch with the moss that grew on it. In the faint moonlight he saw a white shape looming ahead of him. He strained his eyes and at last made out the shape of a man. A man dressed in a white night shirt. A rope was fastened under his armpits and he was hanging over the churchyard wall by the rope.

Edward blinked. He took a few steps towards the figure then stopped. The face was ghastly but he knew it.

'Geordie!' he cried. 'It's you, Geordie!'

Geordie didn't reply.

The sailor reached out a hand and grasped the wrist of his friend. 'My, but you're cold, Geordie!' he said. 'It's not like you to be out on a chilly night like this dressed in your nightgown.'

Geordie didn't reply.

Edward Henson rubbed a hand over his eyes. 'Oh, but I was forgetting! You died yesterday! You'd better get back in your coffin, mate, before you catch your death of cold!'

Suddenly the rope went tight and a moment later the

corpse was whisked back over the graveyard wall. There was a muttered conversation and footsteps padding over the grass behind the wall.

Edward straightened his shoulders and seemed suddenly sober. He hurried to the house that stood at the gateway to the graveyard. He rapped on the heavy oak door. A window rattled open. 'Who's there?'

'It's me.'

'Who's me?'

'Edward Henson, from the collier ship *Cushie Butterfield*.'

'What do you want?'

'Are you in charge of this graveyard?'

'I am.'

'Well, I'm here to tell you the dead uns are getting out of the churchyard!'

There was a roar of anger from the man at the window. It slammed shut and he was down at the door a few minutes later. He ran out with a gun and vanished between the shadowy gravestones. Edward Henson heard shots and cries.

He walked wearily up the hill to his lodging house. Without bothering to undress he fell onto his straw mattress next to a snoring sailor, pulled a rough wool blanket over himself and was asleep in no time.

The next night he was drinking his ale a lot more slowly.

'So you saved your friend from the sack-'em-up men, I hear,' the landlord said. He was looking at Edward Henson with a little more respect tonight.

'I did. And I hear they found a trail of blood in the churchyard this morning,' the sailor said. 'They do say the bodysnatchers won't be back in this town for a while.'

'Then I owe you a drink, my friend,' the landlord grinned.

'I'd rather have a bite to eat.' There were no pies on sale tonight.

The landlord leaned forward, his thick hands planted heavily on the wet table. 'They do say the two pie men have vanished. A funny couple of men. Foreigners. From Scotland.'

'Ah!'

'And that pie stall was in the perfect place to watch everything that went on in the churchyard.'

'You mean ...'

'It looks like they may have been the bodysnatchers.'

Edward Henson shuddered and took a long drink of his ale. 'You say they sold the bodies to the doctors?'

'They did. They got four guineas apiece for fresh ones. The doctors can't get enough of them. Why?'

The sailor shook his head and looked into the dregs of his ale. 'I was just wondering about their tasty mutton pies...'

Would you make a good bodysnatcher?

The three leading members of a Scottish bodysnatching gang were known as The Spoon, The Mole, and Merry Andrew. Merry Andrew cheated the other two out of some bodysnatching money and they were angry. They planned their revenge. Merry Andrew's sister, Sarah, had just died and they planned to snatch her body and sell it to the doctors.

Imagine you are Merry Andrew. You guess what your partners are up to. What are you going to do about it ...

a) You can report The Spoon and The Mole to the law officers. A watch will be kept on your dear sister's grave. As soon as the bodysnatching villains appear, the law officers will appear and stop them, Sarah can rest in peace and the wicked plan is ruined.

b) You can watch the graveyard. When The Mole and The Spoon appear you can go off to fetch the law officers. The bodysnatchers will be caught in the act. They will have sweated for nothing and they will probably go to jail. Poor beloved Sarah will have been disturbed, but it is worth it to see them locked away.

c) You can hide in the graveyard alone. When The Spoon and The Mole have dug up your sister you can leap out of hiding, dressed in a white sheet, pretending to be a ghost and scare them off. You can put your sister back and cover up her grave again. The villains won't be back and Sarah will be safe.

d) You can hide in the graveyard alone. When The Spoon and The Mole have dug up your sister you can leap out of hiding, dressed in a white sheet, pretending to be a ghost and scare them off. You can take your darling Sarah's body to the surgeon and sell her. The Mole and the Spoon have done the work, you collect the money ... if you can bear to sell your own sister, of course.

Which of the above would you do?
Which did Merry Andrew do?

Answer: d) Merry Andrew sold his sister's body to the surgeons. He even chased The Mole and The Spoon away from the cart they had waiting. He borrowed it to get his sister to the surgeon. He enjoyed telling the story and always had a good laugh. 'The Spoon went without his porridge that night!' he'd chuckle.

If you answered d), and you have a sister, then someone should warn her about you!

75

Quaint quack doctors

The more bodies the doctors cut up the more they learned about the human body. But there was still a lot of ignorance about sickness and disease and many people still took curious cures for their problems.

Newspapers were packed with adverts for curious cures. The following advert is invented but the cures offered are all real Georgian medicines.

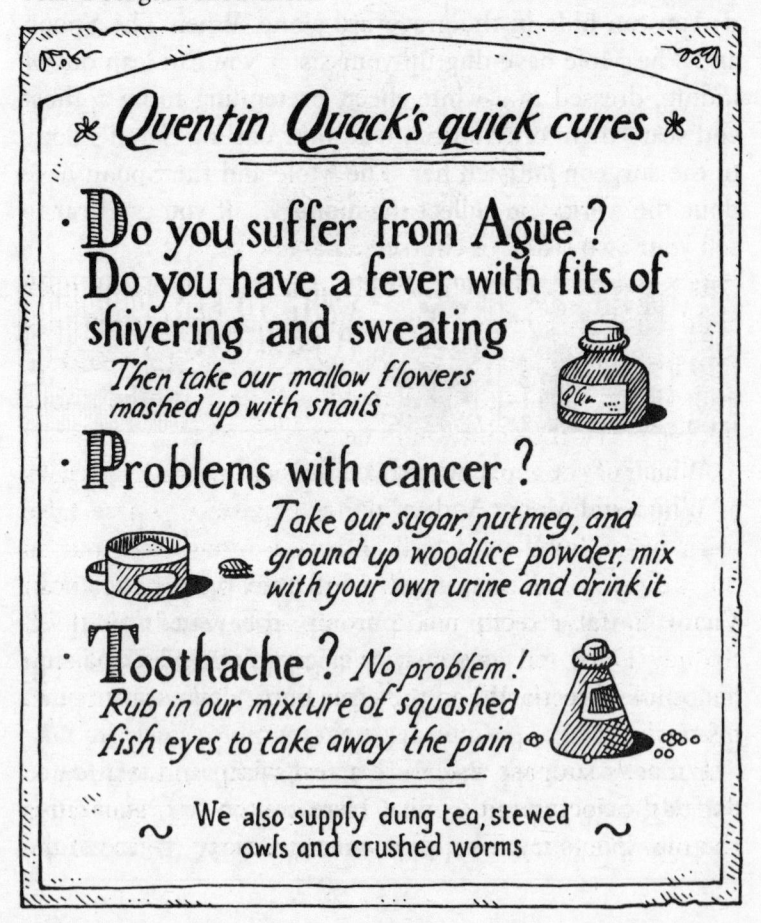

Quentin Quack's quick cures

· **D**o you suffer from Ague? Do you have a fever with fits of shivering and sweating
Then take our mallow flowers mashed up with snails

· **P**roblems with cancer?
Take our sugar, nutmeg, and ground up woodlice powder, mix with your own urine and drink it

· **T**oothache? *No problem!*
Rub in our mixture of squashed fish eyes to take away the pain

~ We also supply dung tea, stewed owls and crushed worms ~

Dodge the doctor

Some people didn't fancy visiting their doctor or dentist – especially the dentist. Yet the dentists were no worse than they are today.

They would invite you to lie on the floor and strap you down. Then they would kneel over you with your head between their legs, say, 'We'll have this out in no time!' and get to work. Just like your dentist, eh? What on earth is there to be afraid of?

If you were really rich then the dentist could have a poor child lying beside you. As soon as your bad tooth was whipped out (or ripped out) a good 'live' tooth would be pulled from the child and planted in the gap in your gums. (Don't worry, the child would be paid!)

Other toothless patients had false teeth made from tusks of hippopotamus or walrus or from pottery. These false teeth never fitted very well and were often taken out so the wearer could eat a meal. (Still they were better than Victorian false teeth made from rubber and celluloid. Sydney Dark fell asleep with a cigar clamped between his celluloid teeth. When the cigar burnt down it set fire to his teeth!)

But let's suppose you were a real wimp and wanted to dodge the doctor and dentist. Here are ten Georgian cures you may like to try. There's just one problem ... nine of the crazy cures were actually tried by the Georgians. One has been made up and was never used by the Georgians – or anyone else. Can you spot which is the odd one out ...

1 James Woodforde had a sty on his eyelid. He heard that it would go if he rubbed it with the tail of a black cat. He tried it ... and it worked!

2 Thomas Grey's friend suffered from swollen joints and heard that boiling a whole chicken and eating it with six litres of beer would cure him. He tried it ... and it worked!

3 People bitten by a mad dog could catch the dog's disease, rabies. The cure was to take a hair from the dog and put it on the wound or swallow it ... this never worked.

4 Toothache is easily cured. Take a poker and heat it in the fire. When it is nice and hot then burn the ear lobe with the poker and the pain in the tooth will go away.

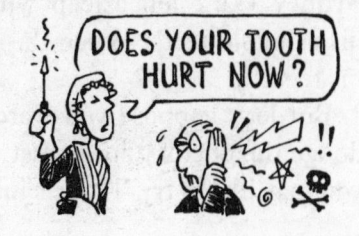

5 Lavinia Cordle found that a boil on her bottom was painful. Bursting it with a needle caused the boil to spread. Her friend said the trick was to burst it suddenly. Lavinia lifted her skirts and bent over with her back to a horse. Her friend tickled the horse's leg with a stalk of straw. When the kick of the horse landed on Lavinia's backside, the boil burst. The iron of the horse's hoof helped the sore spot to heal in half the time. Lavinia was able to sit down within a month – as soon as the bruise from the kick went away.

6 Bad breath caused by rotten teeth could be a problem. (You can tell if you have bad breath – friends like to chat to you from the far end of a football pitch with a megaphone.) The Georgians believed the best cure was to scrape the skin off a turnip, roast the pieces and wear them behind the ear.

7 Another Georgian cure for rabies was said to be a bath in salt water or, even better, a dunk in the sea. A man from Bristol was bitten and taken out to sea in a boat. He said, 'I'll never survive the dip in the sea!' They dipped him anyway and pulled him back into the boat, where he immediately died.

8 A wasp sting inside the throat can kill you. The Georgians believed that you should swallow the juice of an onion to cure a sting like that. It may save your life. And the wasp will buzz off with its eyes full of tears. (Of course the best cure is not to go around with your mouth open.)

9 An adder sting is nasty ... and the Georgian cure was nastier! In 1821 a woman was bitten by an adder near Southampton and was a long way from a doctor. The local people took a chicken, killed it and placed its warm guts over the wound. Sounds *foul*, but they said it worked.

10 Smallpox had killed many people through the ages but the Georgians found a way of preventing it – vaccination. They actually gave people a cattle sickness called cow pox. The cow pox didn't harm them but it did keep the smallpox sickness away.

Answer: 5. The other crazy cures were all really tired. And number **10,** vaccination, is a brilliant Georgian invention that has led to thousands of modern cures and saved millions of lives.

Bedlam, blood, blisters and baths

If you had problems with your mind it was a dreadful life for you in Georgian times. Mentally ill people were called 'mad' and locked away. Treatments included …

• being beaten
• being thrown into cold baths
• being made to vomit
• having blood let out of the body.

The most famous Georgian to suffer mental illness was King George III. So-called treatments included …

• fastening him to his bed

I NEED TO SCRATCH MY NOSE!

• shouting at him – after stuffing handkerchiefs in the king's mouth so he couldn't answer back

WHY CAN'T I STUFF THE HANDKERCHIEFS IN MY EARS?

- forming blisters on his head then bursting them – to let the badness out of his head

- giving him medicines that made him so sick he prayed to be cured or dead.

George's joke
George's behaviour was strange but he wasn't stupid. He was visited by a new doctor, Doctor Willis, and he hated the man on sight. The king questioned the man ...

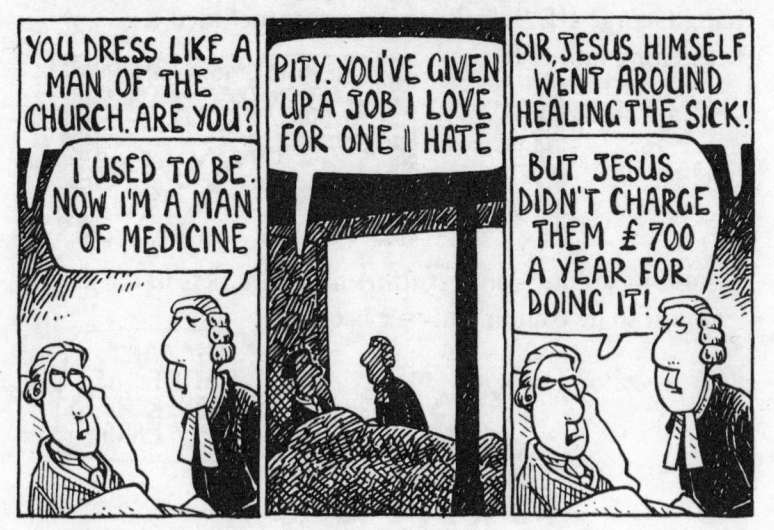

In fact Willis was later paid £10,000 (over half a million pounds at today's value) to treat mad Queen Maria of Portugal. He failed to cure her but was paid anyway.

Still, George could have been treated worse! Ordinary people in London's Bethlehem Hospital (known as Bedlam for short) were chained in their cells if they had mental problems. The porters in charge of the hospital made extra pocket money – they let the public look into the cells to 'give them cause for laughter' and charged a penny.

Gory Georgian fun and games

The people of Georgian Britain liked to enjoy themselves in great crowds. They flocked to fairs and packed into parks, thronged theatres and crowded coffee shops.

Of course Georgians didn't have televisions to amuse them. But maybe you'd swap a night's television for the fun of the Georgian fair? You could see ...

- Miller the German Giant (other 'freak shows' included 'a girl of 15 with strange moles on her backside')
- Violante the acrobat
- a conjuror
- a waxworks display
- a fire-eater
- a performing dog
- a dancing horse
- a slack-rope walker (unless he'd had a bit too much to drink, in which case he'd become a 'tight' rope walker). Slack-rope walker Madame Margaretta stood on one leg on a rope and balanced 13 full glasses on a tobacco pipe.

There were one or two horrors you might not enjoy so much, like ...

- bear-baiting (the bear was chained to a post. Spectators paid a shilling each to set their dogs on the bear.)
- badger-baiting
- cock fights (often arranged in village churchyards!)
- goose-riding (a goose was hung from a tree by its feet. Riders would gallop underneath it and try to snatch its head off. This was made difficult by greasing the bird's beak.)

Any sort of cruelty to animals was enjoyed by some people. One advert announced ...

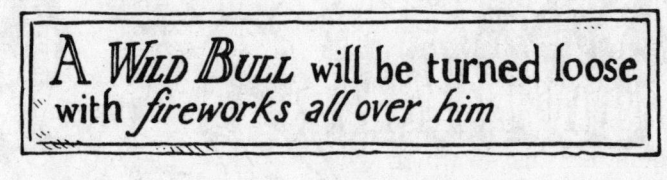

A *WILD BULL* will be turned loose with *fireworks all over him*

Not quite so bad was cruelty to humans at a fair which advertised ...

A player of bagpipes

There were also fights between women. A foreign visitor called Cesar de Sassure described one …

> *Both women wore very little clothing. One was a stout Irishwoman and the other a small Englishwoman, full of fire and very nippy. The weapons were a sort of blunt, two-handed sword. Presently the Irishwoman received a cut across the forehead and that put a stop to the first part of the fight. The Englishwoman's supporters threw money and cheered for her. During this time the wounded woman's forehead was sewn up, this being done on stage, she drank a large glass of spirits and the fight began again. The Irishwoman was wounded a second time then a third time with a long and deep wound all across her neck and throat. A few coins were thrown to her but the winner made a good income from the fight.*

In another fight two women fought a 'boxing and scratching match' till their faces were covered in blood and their clothes torn off their bodies. It sounds a bit like a girls' hockey match today, only not so violent.

In a London club a man fought three women at the same time and knocked them all out.

De Sassure went on to describe men fighting with the same weapons. The loser's ear was almost cut from his head.

A public notice appeared in Gateshead in County Durham on 22 May 1758. It read …

On this day
the annual ENTERTAINMENTS
at Swalwell Fair will take place
This will consist of …

~ Dancing for ribbons

~ Women running for smocks

~ Ass races

~ Foot races for men

~ With the odd whim of a man eating a
cockerel alive, feathers, entrails and all !!!

In Cambridge in 1770 a 16-year-old boy 'ate a whole cat smothered with onions.' But at least the cat was dead and cooked!

Sports and games you may not want to play
1 Fighting animals Eating a live chicken sounds cruel but cock-fighting was still a popular sport and bull-baiting was watched by huge crowds. In some places it was finally stopped when spectators were injured. The magistrates

didn't stop it because they were worried about the cruelty to the animals. Rich people, like the Duke of Cumberland, got pleasure from setting a tiger to kill a stag … in a 1764 contest the stag won.

2 Horse racing Horse racing could be cruel. Horses raced time and again in heats as long as four miles. The exhausted horse that won the most heats was the winner.

There was also cruelty to jockeys – they were fond of barging, pushing and whipping their opponents. A writer said …

> *I remember one jockey who used to boast of the damage he did by striking with the handle of his whip. He liked to describe the number of eyes and the teeth he had beaten out.*

A lot of money was gambled on horse races and some gamblers were bad losers. They sometimes set upon a jockey with sticks and stones and whips!

3 Soccer Football games were often organized in the street. Two sides booted a leather ball filled with air and weren't too bothered about how many windows they broke in houses and coaches. In Gloucester in 1811 the *Shrewsbury Chronicle* reported ...

An apprentice was convicted of playing football on a Sunday. He was sentenced to 14 days in prison.

Nowadays he'd be paid £10,000 a week and sentenced to play 90 minutes a week! (That's about £1.85 a second.)

4 Cricket In 1748 a court finally decided that another dreadfully dangerous game was actually legal – though people had been playing it for hundreds of years. This weird game was called 'cricket.' Teams of men (with some women players in London) threw a hard ball at some wooden pegs. The players wore no pads or gloves so broken bones, torn fingernails and bleeding injuries were common. A farmer was killed by a cricket ball in 1825. Maybe a return to Georgian cricket would liven the sport up today! Or this unusual Surrey match of 1773 ...

Last Wednesday an extraordinary match of cricket was played on Guildford Downs between a carpenter on one side and nine tailors on the other side. The prize was a quarter of lamb and a cabbage. The match was won by the Carpenter by 64 runs.

What a pity that Georgian carpenter isn't around to play for England's cricket team today. In 1997 England's cricketers lost to Matabeleland and Zimbabwe – in Britain in 1770 nobody had even heard of Matabeleland and Zimbabwe!

5 Hunting The deer hunting of earlier times went out of fashion and fox-hunting became the most popular entertainment for the upper classes. Hare hunting was popular too because hares didn't run so far.1 In 1790 a hare actually escaped from the pack and the *Newcastle Chronicle* reported ...

The hare fled and, with a wonderful leap, darted through a pane of glass in a window of The Globe Inn. It landed amongst a pile of legal papers since the inn was crowded with lawyers at the time. As soon as they recovered from the shock, the lawyers presented the poor hare to the cook ...

You'd think the lawyers would have given it a fair hare trial, wouldn't you? But that's life. Hare today, gone tomorrow.

6 Rugby In 1823 two teams of boys were playing football at Rugby school when William Webb Ellis picked up the ball and ran with it. This new idea became quite popular (it gives your feet a rest) and the school had invented a new ball game! What should they call it? William–Webb–Ellis–Ball?

1. Popular for ladies and gentlemen, that is. Two boys who killed a hare for food were given a public whipping in Reading in 1773.

No. How about Pick-it-up-and-run-with-it-till-somebody-jumps-on-you-ball? That's better.

STRANGE... IT SEEMS TO HAVE GOT DARK

7 Ballooning In Newcastle Upon Tyne, there was a report of a new entertainment in 1786. An old history book told the story …

Mr Lunardi, the famous aeronaut, made an attempt to ascend in an air balloon from the river bank. In filling it Mr Lunardi added the last of the acid and the hot steam became remarkably strong and thick. This gave so much alarm to those on that side of the balloon, who thought that it was on fire, that they immediately let go of their side of the net. The balloon being free on one side made a sudden stretch upwards. The balloon, set free,

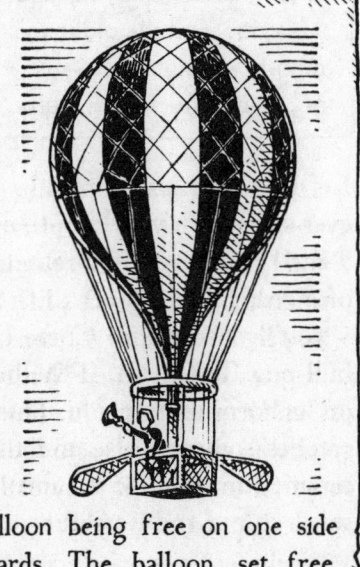

ascended rapidly and dragged with it Master Ralph Heron. The boy had one of the balloon ropes twisted round his hand and arm. When he reached a height of 500 feet the rope snapped off the balloon and he fell into a nearby garden. He died soon after.

8 Chuckstones This game involves throwing up stones and catching them on the back of the hand. It's been popular since ancient times but two Georgian boys came up with a new version in 1760. You could call it 'kill-a-wrinkly' …

In a small Devon village an old labouring man, John Wilson, was lying on a bench fast asleep. Some boys were playing at 'chuckers' and the old man's mouth being open, one of them chucked a stone directly into his mouth. This woke him, but the stone stuck in his throat and choked him before help could be brought. The man was over 90 years old and had never had any sickness.

Let that be a lesson to all you chuckstone players. Never, ever sleep with your mouth open.

9 Bull running Put a rather angry bull in a pen at the end of a road, then go off to the local tavern for a few drinks – you'll need them. Come back and open the gate of the bull pen. Then run. If the bull catches you it will toss you on its horns or gore you. This is no fun at all. But if the bull catches someone else and throws them up in the air it is terrific fun. In 1785 a Lincoln newspaper grumbled that it was a stupid and wasteful sport …

> It is just an excuse for drunkenness and idleness. Even if a man escapes bodily hurt his family is harmed because of the money he spends.

10 Pinching matches Two people stand toe to toe and pinch one another. The one who can stand it the longest is the winner. If a player gets angry or starts to swear then he or she is the loser.

IT'S ALL RIGHT SIS, YOU CAN GO FIRST

The *Hertfordshire Mercury* reporter described a contest between a 'puny' little man and a 'stout' man …

> They kept pinching each other for an hour, chiefly on the flesh parts of the arm. At the end of that time the stout man's arms fell powerless to his side and he had to give in from exhaustion and pain. The puny man offered to fight any man in England for the pinching championship.

... and games you definitely wouldn't want to play

1 A newspaper report of 1818 described this game that turned into gore ...

> On Saturday three boys were playing in a field where some cows were feeding. One of them, about 16 years of age, suggested that they tie another to the tail of a cow. But the enraged animal dragged the victim up and down the field at full speed, plunging in all directions. Before he could be rescued his life was totally extinct.

2 Apple bobbing is popular today but one Georgian invented 'silver bobbing'. A silver coin was dropped into a tub of water and players had to pick it up using their teeth. If you think apple bobbing's hard then don't try this.

3 In 1764 a bored lord in Huntingdon invented a game called 'hunting the hen'. The players had their hands muffled in thick bandages. They had to catch a hen and pull a feather out. The first to take a feather won the hen.

Did you know …?

A man called Jedediah Buxton travelled the country, entertaining people as a mathematical wonder. Jed had never been taught to read or write but he was famous for his maths skills. He was once asked to work out how many hairs' breadths (at 48 hairs to the inch) it would take to reach from Tyneside to London. He answered in less than three minutes (and without a pocket calculator) 833,310,720. And that, give or take a few curls, is about right!

WHEN ARE PEOPLE AROUND HERE GOING TO LEARN HOW TO SPELL?

A game you might like to play
A jingling match
This was a popular game played by women at fairs and can be played by a class of pupils in a school hall, yard or field.

You need:
• a bell on a string
• 12 scarves.

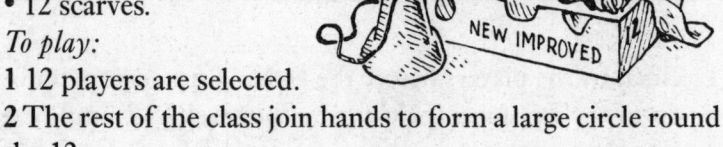

To play:

1 12 players are selected.

2 The rest of the class join hands to form a large circle round the 12.

3 One player – the Jingler – has the bell hung round her (or his) neck and her hands tied behind her with a scarf.

4 The other 11 players have scarves tied over their eyes.

5 The blindfolded players try to catch the Jingling player who can move anywhere in the circle to escape.

6 If the Jingler escapes for one minute then he or she wins.

7 If a blindfolded player catches the jingler then he or she wins and becomes the Jingler.

A jingling match

Prizes:

Decided by the players before the game. A new computer or a trip to the Bahamas (paid for by the teacher) would be a reasonable sort of prize.

Wacky Georgian words

The language we use is forever changing. Old words are forgotten or get new meanings and new ones are invented. Georgian Britain was no different.

Forgotten words include *odsbodikins* (a swear word) and *hock-dockies* for shoes. What a sad loss they are.

Changed words included *respectable* to mean polite. (And the Georgians tried to be polite. They used fewer swear words. No *respectable* person said *belly* or *bitch* any longer.)

The bill for food at a tavern was called the *scran*. It changed in Georgian times to mean the food itself … and it still does.

New words came along with new fashions. A man in Georgian times could often be judged by the size of his hair-piece. So what did they call a very important man? A *bigwig* of course.

If you are going to understand the Georgians you probably need to know some of their words.

Match the following words to their meanings …

1. A blue pigeon flier	*a. is an idiot*
2. A louse trap	*b. is a coat*
3. A sumph	*c. is a horse*
4. A wooden suit	*d. is a gossip*
5. A daisy-kicker	*e. is a comb*
6. A magpie	*f. is a neck*
7. A cover-me-queerly	*g. is a thief who steals the lead off your roof*
8. A sad man	*h. is a coffin*
9. A tattle box	*i. is a trouble-maker*
10. A scrag	*j. is a small coin*

Answers:

1g) *Blue pigeon* is lead, probably because of the colour.

2e) Obvious when you think about it. Similar to the delightful modern phrase 'nit rake'.

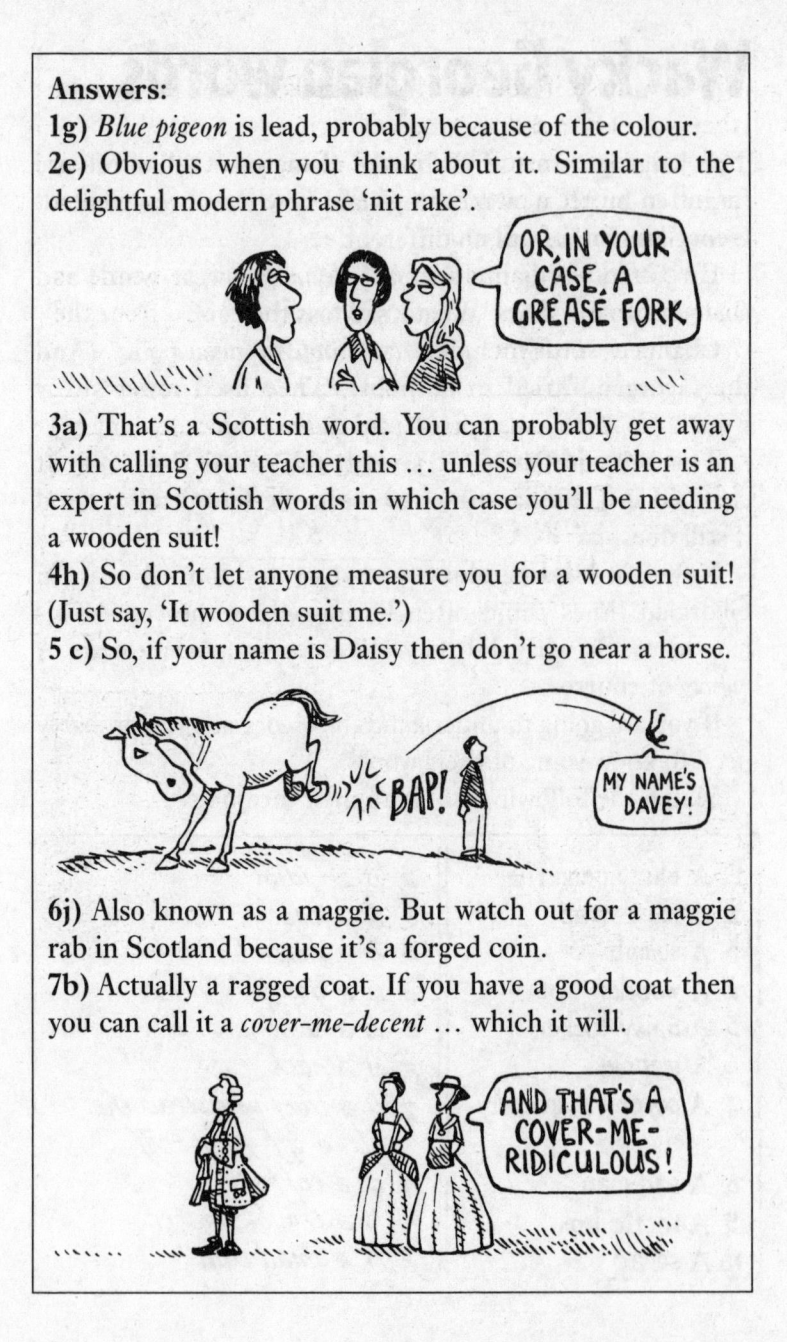

OR, IN YOUR CASE, A GREASE FORK

3a) That's a Scottish word. You can probably get away with calling your teacher this ... unless your teacher is an expert in Scottish words in which case you'll be needing a wooden suit!

4h) So don't let anyone measure you for a wooden suit! (Just say, 'It wooden suit me.')

5 c) So, if your name is Daisy then don't go near a horse.

BAP!

MY NAME'S DAVEY!

6j) Also known as a maggie. But watch out for a maggie rab in Scotland because it's a forged coin.

7b) Actually a ragged coat. If you have a good coat then you can call it a *cover-me-decent* ... which it will.

AND THAT'S A COVER-ME-RIDICULOUS!

8i) Of course if you're a troublemaker who gets caught then you'll be a sad, sad man.

9d) Just like a match box is full of matches, a lunch box is full of lunch, a tattle-box is full of tattle. So why isn't a pillar-box full of pillars?

10f) The Georgian meaning of *scragging* someone is hanging them. So, a scrag boy would hang you from the *scragging-post* till your scrag was totally *scragged*!

Rotten revolutions

Britain has always suffered from riots. The Georgians seemed to suffer more than most.

A writer said …

> *I have seen this year riots in the country about corn; riots about elections; riots about workhouses; riots of miners, riots of weavers, riots of wood-cutters; and I have seen riots of smugglers in which law officers have been murdered and the king's troops fired at.*

And this was in 1769. Twenty years later the French had a terrifying revolution where the king and the nobles were executed. The Georgians feared the same could happen over here. It never did, but the British went to war with the French Emperor who replaced the headless king, Emperor Napoleon Bonaparte.

Napoleon expected the British people to support a revolution – after all, there had been all of those riots. When he sent French soldiers to help a British revolution he got a surprise …

Mum's army

In 1797 a French force of 1,400 soldiers landed on the Welsh coast and they expected the local people to help them. They thought there would be a Welsh Revolution that would drive out the evil English. The defence of Britain rested on Lord Cawdor of Stackpole Hall.

If Lord Cawdor had written to a friend of the time he may have admitted that his victory was a great surprise – to the British defenders more than the French attackers!

My dear Thomas,

You have probably heard the tale of the French invasion of Wales by now. But the truth is even stranger than the reports that have appeared in the newspapers. Of course they say I'm a hero, but to tell the truth I had some unexpected luck.

I was having supper at Stackpole Hall when a messenger arrived on a horse that was foaming with sweat and more dead than alive. 'Lord Cawdor!' he cried. 'The French have arrived!'

'What? Here? Now?' I asked. 'They're just in time for supper.'

'No!' he groaned. 'Thousands of them have landed at Fishguard! They're raiding every farm in the area. They're stealing every drop of wine they can find.'

'Anyone been hurt?' I asked.

'Not exactly.' the man shrugged. 'They're a bit nervous. They're shooting at anything that moves. Huw Thomas at Pencaer Farm said one of the. French soldiers came into his parlour and heard a noise behind him. He turned and fired wildly.'

'Did he hit anyone?'

'No but he wrecked Huw's grandfather clock. That's what was making the noise, you see?'

I couldn't believe what I was hearing, Thomas. 'So, we have a couple of thousand scared Frenchmen shooting our clocks. And you've ridden 30 miles to tell me this? It's Colonel Knox you should be telling. He's the man in charge of the local defence force, the Fishguard Fencibles.'

'Colonel Knox was at a ball when he got the news. He said "The Fishguard Fencibles are no match for a French army." He decided to retreat.'

I can tell you, Thomas. I almost exploded with rage. 'He ran away!'

'He retreated, sir.' the miserable messenger said.

'Then the Stackpole Yeomanry will have to show him how its done', I said.

I guess it took less than an hour for the men to come in from the surrounding villages, gather their weapons and meet at Stackpole Hall. Of course everyone had heard about the invasion and my men were ready for them. We set off for Haverfordwest the next morning, camped there and gathered more men, then set off for Fishguard the day after. I suppose we had 500 men in all by the time we spotted the French camp.

Now my men were spoiling for a fight, but it was clear the French outnumbered us. So I sent a message to their commander. 'My forces are growing stronger every hour. Surrender now or you will be wiped out.' It was a lie, of course, but the commander's reply was the last thing I expected.

The French commander was actually one of those rebel American fellows. A man called William Tate. His reply said, 'We surrender on condition that the men you have already captured are set free.'

I accepted his surrender and met him at Fishguard harbour to take his men's weapons and accept the surrender. And that's when I told him, 'We haven't actually captured any of your men.'

The American shook his head and pointed up the main street. 'Your British Army red-coats took 20 of our men. The rest of the French were so drunk they ran away when the red-coats attacked.'

Now I knew that the nearest red-coat army was still 40 miles away in Carmarthen. But when I looked along the harbour I saw 20 French soldiers trooping along looking very sorry for themselves. And they weren't being held by red-coats... they were being marched along by red cloaks! A little group of women were wearing their red Welsh cloaks and those tall black hats they have in this country. They were armed with pitch-forks and reaping hooks and they had the French terrified.

The woman in charge strode across to me. A huge woman – she certainly terrified me. She threw a huge salute and grinned. 'Mistress Jemima Nicholas at your service', she said.

It seems the French had made the mistake of trying to attack these women and they'd been taken prisoner instead. The rest of the

French invaders had lost heart and persuaded Tate to surrender.

So there you have it! They say the Stackpole Yeomanry and I are the heroes. The truth is the mighty Jemima Nicholas and the women of Fishguard have saved our country from the invaders. Her name should go down in history with heroines like Boudicca and Queen Elizabeth.

God save the King, and God bless you too my friend.   yours Robert Lord Cawdor

Everybody remembers the first French invasion – they remember King Harold the hero who died with an arrow in his eye. But he was a man and a king so he's remembered even though he lost.

Sadly Jemima Nicholas and the Pembroke 'Mum's Army' have been almost forgotten. She was a woman, of course, and it doesn't seem to matter that she actually won! (You could be reading this in French if she hadn't!)

After this defeat the French never tried invading Britain again. In fact no invader has landed on Britain's shores since. (Unless you count a few German pilots shot down in World War II.)

During the Napoleonic Wars Lord Nelson and the navy protected the British from attack by sea. Then British armies crossed to the continent and finally defeated the French at the Battle of Waterloo in 1815.

A few troublemakers tried to copy the French Revolution in Britain, but they didn't get much support. George III kept his head.

The American Revolution

Of course the British had another Revolution to worry about. They had some colonies on the far side of the Atlantic Ocean in a place called America. It had been a good place to dump convicts at one time.

But in the reign of George III those American Colonists started to get stroppy. They weren't happy with being told what to do by a king and a parliament back in Britain. They wanted to make their own decisions – they wanted to be free to kill Native Americans and steal their land, free to invent hamburgers and free to play cowboys. But above all, they wanted to be free of paying tax to Britain.

Not everybody in America wanted to be a rebel, of course. But the Americans who tried to stay loyal to Britain could be given a tough time.

The diary of a rebel tells what happened to one American soldier who disagreed with his rebel friends …

8 August 1775.
        Riflemen took a man in New Milford
who had called them 'damned rebels' and
other insulting names. They made him walk

in front of them to Litchfield, a journey of 20 miles. He was made to carry one of his geese in his hand all the way. When they arrived there they covered him in tar and made him pluck his goose. They stuck the feathers to him, drummed him out of the rifle company, forced him to kneel down and thank them for being so merciful to him.

(The writer of the diary doesn't say what happened to the goose, but they probably cut it up, covered it in batter and fried it – another American invention: *Litchfield Fried Goose*, perhaps?)

In the end America got the freedom they wanted. Britain couldn't fight a war at a distance of 3,000 miles. They created a new country – the United States of America – and elected a president instead of a king. They picked a leading rebel fighter, George Washington, to be the first President.

Back in Britain poor old George III was the loser – he lost the American Colonies and went on to lose his marbles.

The Luddite revolts
The Industrial Revolution meant that one man and a machine could do the work of (maybe) ten men. It meant that nine men were put out of work. They were not a happy nine men. Some of the nine believed that the answer was to smash up the machine!

(This does not make a lot of sense. One horse could do the work of ten men – pulling a plough, say – but you didn't see farm workers going around beating up horses, did you?)

Trouble started in 1811 in Yorkshire and spread through Nottinghamshire and Lancashire. Machine breakers gathered in gangs and marched like an army to destroy machines. The army was called in to defend the machines with guns – the machine-wreckers armed themselves with guns. Many died in the battles that followed.

Machine owners who tried to defend themselves were murdered – the murderers were hanged – the youngest to hang was a boy of 15 and the oldest a man of nearly 70. These machine smashers were called Luddites because they were said to follow the mighty machine-breaker, Ned Ludd. 'Disobey Ned Ludd and you die!'

The very name brought fear to the hearts of the mill-owners, mothers used the name to scare their children: 'Behave yourself or Ned Ludd will get you!'

But who was this Ned Ludd? The truth is he was never a rebel leader. This is what happened …

The truth is the Luddites never had any leader. Each group was dealt with by the army one at a time and the Luddite riots died as quickly as they had started.

If they'd had a single, strong leader it might have been different, but they never had one. They certainly never had one called Ned Ludd – and Ned Ludd was never a Luddite.

The Peterloo massacre

The machine wreckers went quiet for a long time while the war against Napoleon came to its bloody end at the Battle of Waterloo in 1815.

But soldiers came home to a Britain where corn prices were getting higher and wages were getting lower. When that happens, of course, you get hungry … and you get angry.

By 1819 the people of the north were particularly angry.

A huge meeting was called at Saint Peter's Fields near Manchester. Workers and their families came from all over the north to hear the famous Henry Hunt speak about the changes the workers wanted. Above all they wanted to vote for members of parliament.

Sixty thousand people packed into the fields till, someone said, 'their hats were almost touching.'

But the magistrates of the area panicked. They called in soldiers to keep the crowds in order. But, in the front line, were the part-time soldiers – local men who were not very well trained but enjoyed wearing the uniforms and swaggering around. Their regiment was called The Manchester and Salford Yeomanry Cavalry – the MYC for short.

In France the angry people turned against the nobles. But in Britain they turned against each other. That was the difference.

Workers didn't like the Prince of Wales who ruled the country while his father was mentally ill. But they really, really hated men like Tom Shelmerdine ... one of their own people who tried to stop their peaceful protest.

If Tom Shelmerdine had kept a diary then it may have looked like this. The diary is imaginary, only the sad facts are true ...

Tom Shelmerdine's diary

Workers gathering into a union to get higher wages was against the law in 1819. Many workers wanted to change the law but they couldn't gather together to protest against because it was against the law to gather together and protest!

Some tried. But Tom Shelmerdine of Manchester wasn't one of them ...

> 21 May 1819 Some of the men in the weaving mill are traitors. I'm sure they're planning to form one of those trade union things. Of course they don't tell me. They think I'll report them and have them arrested. They're right. I would.

For the workers who didn't want to join a union there was something else they could do ...

> 27 May 1819 I'll join the loyal subjects of King George and put a stop to the mill-workers' treason

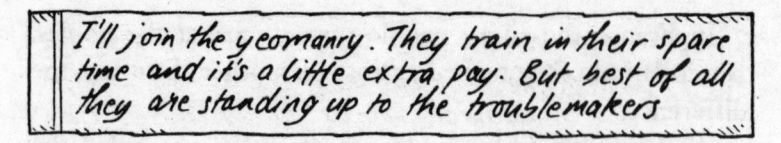

> I'll join the yeomanry. They train in their spare time and it's a little extra pay. But best of all they are standing up to the troublemakers

The local guard regiments were amateurs. A bit like boy scouts with big swords ...

> 9 June 1819 Joined the MYC. I look very smart in the uniform though I say it myself. A nice blue with white trim. Yes, very smart Of course I'm not very good on a horse, but none of the other lads of the MYC are either

In the summer of 1819 the workers of the north planned a peaceful protest. The leaders taught the protesters how to march in formation. They wanted this protest to look really well organized – not just a mob. But the magistrates and the law officers got the wrong idea entirely ...

> 27 June 1819 The weavers have started marching. They are practising drill like an army. The MYC lads reckon they are planning an attack. The yeomanry send their swords away to be polished every month. But this time they've sent them to be sharpened. I keep falling off my brute of a horse.

A meeting planned for 60,000 people couldn't be kept a secret from the magistrates for long, of course ...

> 13 July 1819 Major Trafford, our commander, has told us the rebel secret. They are planning a meeting. The trouble-maker Henry Hunt will

> be at this meeting and he'll be stirring them up.
> The lads of the MYC will be there as well, we hope,
> with our sharpened swords. Harry Bardon cut
> himself at last night's practice.

On the morning of 16 August 1819 the workers gathered all over the north and began marching to St Peter's Fields for the great meeting. Meanwhile the full time soldiers, the Hussars, gathered in Manchester. The part-time soldiers, the MYC, gathered in the local pubs! Giving big swords to boy scouts is not a good idea. Giving big swords and strong drink to boy scouts is stupid. But that's what Hugh Hornby Birley did with the MYC ...

> 16 August 1819 Sixty thousand traitors in
> St Peter's Fields, they reckon. The MYC are in
> this public house and ready. Mr Hugh Hornby
> Birley is buying us as much ale as we want.
> They say the rebels in St Peter's Fields are
> quiet and orderly. But we think that's just a
> trick. When the signal comes we'll be ready. Here
> it is now! The constables are going to arrest
> Henry Hunt! And the MYC, not the hussars,
> have been chosen to escort them.
> To horse Lads!

Of course a lot of the drunken MYC had trouble climbing on their horses, never mind staying on them. The crowds were packed into the field. The constables struggled to get through to Hunt on the platform. So the gallant MYC drew their sabres and hacked their way through. The rest is horrible history ...

17 August 1819 It's over. It was exciting, I think, but I don't remember too much about it. I do remember we galloped onto the field and you should have seen those traitors panic! They'd have run away if they hadn't been so crowded together. They started to scream and that was a big mistake. Well, I mean, it panicked the horses and they went wild. Some of us have enough trouble with a quiet horse. Imagine how dangerous we were on scared horses. I came face to face with old Meg Willis. She recognised me, of course, because she used to nurse me as a child. 'Nay Tom Shelmerdine, thee will not hurt me, I know!' she said. Of course I wouldn't. But the horse did, the brutish animal. Still, it has to be said, if old Meg hadn't been there then she wouldn't have been killed.

Tom Shelmerdine was remembered, and hated, because of the way he rode down the old woman who used to nurse him. Other MYC riders struck out wildly with their sharp sabres. They cut their way through the crowds to get to Hunt. It was a bit like boy scouts cutting their way through a tangled wood – but it wasn't bushes they were hacking at – they were human beings.

18 August 1819 There's a lot of bad feeling about that St. Peter's Fields business. The newspapers are mocking us for charging at unarmed men, women and children. But we

> *didn't know they were unarmed, did we? They could have been hiding pikes under their coats couldn't they? Heroes of Peterloo they are calling us. They forget, we were only doing our job.*

It was the magistrates who sent in the half-trained, half-baked, half-witted MYC when they could have sent in the Hussars. The Hussars went in later and struck people with the flat of their swords to drive them back. The MYC had used the edge of their swords to kill and wound. It's the MYC who were remembered and hated – the local men. These rebels didn't blame the government so much as the French had. They blamed the people they knew. People like Tom Shelmerdine.

So 'Peterloo' killed 11 people and wounded 500.

Peterloo foul facts
- The MYC were sent in to protect the police. But several police were trampled by the rampaging yeomanry. Special Constable Thomas Ashworth died.
- One of the men at the meeting had taken a cheese for his dinner. He stored it under his hat. It saved his life when a sabre chopped at his head!

- A weaver called John Lees had lived through the horror of the Battle of Waterloo and Napoleon's powerful army. But at Peterloo he was cut by a sabre, smashed by a truncheon and trampled by a horse. He died.

- The youngest victim was William Fildes, a baby in his mother's arms. She was walking along the street when the MYC galloped, out of control, towards St Peter's Fields. The baby was knocked to the ground and trampled. Mrs Fildes wasn't even at the meeting.
- A poet at the meeting described the charge through the crowd: 'Sabres were used to hew a way through held-up hands and defenceless heads; chopped limbs and wound-gaping skulls were seen; groans and cries were mingled with the din of that horrid confusion.'

- Hunt was arrested and taken to Lancaster Jail. On his return from Lancaster his horse, Bob, died near Preston. He was buried under a weeping willow with a headstone that read, 'Alas! Poor Bob!!!' Thousands of people went to the funeral.

- BUT … seven years later Bob's remains were dug up and his bones turned into snuff boxes. A knee-cap was given a silver lid and presented to Hunt.

Instant 'Peterloo' quiz
The government had an enquiry into the massacre. Who got the blame …
a) The magistrates for sending in the MYC
b) The MYC commanders for getting the men drunk
c) The MYC members for being out of control
d) Henry Hunt for arranging the meeting

Answer: d) Of course. What did you expect?

Test your teacher

Teachers love asking questions. They even get paid for it! It would be really boring if every pupil got every question right, so teachers learn to enjoy it when their pupils get the *wrong* answers. Now it's your chance to get your revenge. Test your teacher (or pester your parent) with this amazingly difficult quiz.

When they get a wrong answer you can mutter, 'I thought you'd have known that!'

1 What would a Georgian doctor do with a 'pelican'?
a) Train it to catch fish alive so patients could swallow them and cure swamp fever.
b) Use it to pull out a deeply rooted, rotten tooth.
c) Boil its eggs, grind them up with beetroot and make plague plasters.

2 In 1750 a gentleman bought a pound of tea from a smuggler. He didn't like the look of the tea so he fed it to the dog. What happened next?
a) The dog became a tea addict and had to be fed a saucer every day.

DOG AND BONE CHINA

DOG AND BONE

b) The dog refused to drink it until the gentleman added sugar and milk.

HOW MANY TIMES HAVE I GOT TO TELL YOU, MILK FIRST, *THEN* THE TEA!

c) The dog had a fit and died.

3 What did Robinson Cruso do for a living?
a) He made beds and auctioned furniture.
b) He was a sailor who enjoyed being shipwrecked and writing about it.
c) He was a writer whose most famous book was about a desert island.

4 Carlisle Spedding invented a steel mill – it struck sparks off a flint stone and gave light. Useful for pitmen in a coal mine. But … when it was used in a mine it could explode firedamp gas. It killed a lot of miners. But how did Spedding himself die?
a) His steel mill set fire to his wig.
b) His steel mill failed, he stumbled in the dark and fell in a river.
c) His steel mill caused an explosion of firedamp in a coal mine and killed him.

5 A gentleman in Georgian Britain would not wear what?
a) Trousers.
b) A waistcoat.
c) Stockings.

6 Tearing hares apart with hounds is an ancient sport, enjoyed by the Georgians. But when was it stopped?

a) Not until 1826 in the reign of George IV.

b) Not until 1897 in the reign of Queen Victoria.

c) Not at all. Hare hunting is still legal in Britain.

7 The Georgians spent a lot of time at war with France. They weren't too keen on any foreigners. What did they do to some foreigners on the streets of London?

a) Spat at them.

b) Threw dead cats and dogs at them.

c) Swore at them in French.

8 Sailors in Nelson's navy suffered bad food. The cheese was often too hard to eat, but they had another use for that. What?

a) They used it in mouse traps. The mice broke their teeth on the cheese and starved.

b) The sailors carved the cheese with their knives to make tough, hard wearing buttons for their coats.

c) They used the cheeses to play a game like shove-ha'penny on deck. It was called shove cheddar.

9 What useful thing did the watchmaker Andrew Cumming invent in 1775 that we still use today?

a) A stink trap.

b) Roller skates.

c) Knickers held up with elastic.

10 Highwaymen couldn't always afford pistols. In 1774 a Huntingdon highwayman held up a coach using what?

a) A bow and arrow.

b) A savage dog.

c) A candlestick.

Answers:

1b) A 'pelican' was a tool for pulling out difficult teeth. When pliers failed to remove the tooth, the pelican would rip it out sideways. A careless doctor could rip out good teeth along with the bad. There were even cases of good teeth being torn out and the bad one left! The instrument got its name because it looked like a pelican's beak.

A pelican with some bad teeth

2c) The dog died and the gentleman complained to the local newspaper. Of course the gentleman couldn't complain to the law because he should not have been buying cheap tea from a smuggler. He couldn't complain to the smuggler because no one could trace him. Still, he was lucky. If he'd drunk the tea he wouldn't have complained to anybody – ever again!

3a) Robinson Cruso, a bed-maker, lived in Kings Lynn High Street. The writer Daniel Defoe visited Kings Lynn on his travels and must have seen the name Robinson Cruso outside the shop. Defoe then told the story of shipwrecked sailor Alexander Selkirk and changed his name … to Robeson Cruso. (Later publishers changed the spelling to Robinson Crusoe.) So, next time your parents tell you to 'make your bed' say, 'Who do you think I am? Robinson Crusoe?' That'll confuse them!

STRANGE CHILD

MAYBE IT'S TOO MUCH READING

4c) Carlisle Spedding's invention caused an explosion. Poor old Spedding. Spark – boom! – and Spedding is speeding up a mine-shaft!

5a) Peasants wore trousers to work in the fields and a gentleman would not be so common as to wear them. Gentlemen wore tighter fitting 'breeches' with stockings. Did you guess that? If not it was a turn-up for the books!

6c) That's right. Hare 'coursing' as it's called is still enjoyed today by many people and many packs of hounds. The hares must enjoy it too, otherwise they'd arm themselves with hare-rifles, wouldn't they?

IF THEIR DOG GOT TORN UP, WOULD THEY STILL ENJOY IT?

7b) It makes you wonder where they got the dead cats and dogs from! Were they just lying around in the street for ruffians to pick up and throw when they saw a foreigner? Or did they say, 'Look! A foreigner. Let's kill a cat and throw it! Here pussy, pussy, pussy!'

8b) The biscuits were worse than the cheese. They were full of black-headed maggots. The sailors usually shut their eyes and ate them. I wonder if the maggots shut their eyes as they were about to be eaten?

MY BISCUIT IS WINKING AT ME

9a) A 'stink trap' is a bend in the toilet pipe that stops smells coming up from the drains. Every home should have one. It's a pity no one's invented a stink trap for a team of boys who have been playing football. Phew!

10c) The candlestick may have looked like the barrel of a pistol but the guard on the coach wasn't fooled. He shot the highwayman with a blunderbuss gun and two slugs ended up in the thief's forehead. The candlestick robber was snuffed out. He probably got on the guard's wick.

Epilogue

George I could have travelled through his new kingdom, Britain, in 1714. He'd have bounced along rutted roads and moved very slowly. From his carriage he'd have seen lots of large areas of common ground divided into strips where poor people farmed their own little piece of land. He'd have seen some magnificent houses and some that were not fit for animals.

SCHÖNE AUSSICHT- SCHADE DASS DIE ARMEN LEUTE IM WEG SIND*

* NICE VIEW, SHAME ABOUT THE POOR

If his great-great-grandson George IV had made the same journey over a hundred years later he may have taken one of the new steam trains – they were sooty and noisy and cold but at least they were much faster. And they'd have crossed over those new canal things. The common ground would be mostly gone and there would be fields closed in with hedges and fences now. The poor people who used to live off the common ground would have gone too. Some would have had to go and work for one of the farmers who owned the fields. More would have gone to the towns.

That would be the biggest change. The towns had become huge and crowded; factory smoke blackened the skies and faces of the workers. The factories made Georgian Britain the richest nation on Earth ... and made some lucky people very rich too. The Georgians also left behind a world that was famous for its slums and some unfortunate people who had to live and die in them.

The gorgeous Georgians changed some things for the better – they got rid of slave trading in their country and they avoided the worst horrors of revolutions.

But would *you* like to have lived in Georgian Britain? If you have money, and if you like to make yourself look gorgeous with make-up and wigs and fine clothes, then you might have enjoyed it!

But Georgian Britain is a bit like the moon; it's bright and flashy to look at from a distance … you may even like to visit it … but you wouldn't want to live there.
Would you?

LET'S PLAY GEORGIANS. I GET TO WEAR THE WIG. YOU GET TO BE TRANSPORTED FOR STEALING A SAUSAGE AND DIE OF STARVATION IN SOME FACTORY SOMEWHERE

GORGEOUS GEORGIANS

GRISLY QUIZ

**Now find out if you're a
Gorgeous Georgians expert!**

QUICK GEORGIAN QUESTIONS

This was the age when pirates were the scourge of the seas, highwaymen haunted the roads, a crackpot was king and the Americans were revolting... some things never change. It was also the age of thick make-up, beauty spots, monstrous wigs and padded bosoms – and that was just the men.

1. In 1700 John Asgill went to prison for writing a short book called, A man can go from here to heaven without... Without what? (Clue: everybody does it)

2. In Scotland in 1700 a teacher was whipped through the streets of Edinburgh (don't laugh!). What was his crime? (Clue: tough teacher)

3. In 1707 the son of the Duke of Queensberry murdered a kitchen boy. How did he dispose of the evidence? (Clue: it's in really bad taste)

4. Why did Queen Anne's doctors shave her head and cover her feet in garlic? (Clue: sick idea)

5. Queen Anne died in 1714 and she was buried in a coffin that is almost square. Why? (Clue: if the coffin fits, wear it)

6. German George I took the throne. But where was his wife Dorothea? (Clue: she flirted once too often)

7. In Banff in 1714 the town hangman had to catch stray dogs. He was paid for each dog he caught. How did he prove he'd caught a dog? (Clue: hide!)

8. In 1717 a Scottish teacher murdered two pupils in his charge. Before he was hanged he had an odd punishment. What was it? (Clue: he'd never write on a blackboard again)

9. In 1718 the dreaded pirate Blackbeard was shot and beheaded by a navy officer. Blackbeard's body was thrown over the side of the ship. What's supposed to have happened next? (Clue: maybe he crawled)

10. Many Georgian pirates wore gold earrings. Why? (Clue: go to see?)

11. In 1722 an elephant died on its way to Dundee. What did Doctor Patrick Blair do with the corpse? (Clue: jumbo scientist)

12. In 1724 murderer Maggie Dickson escaped execution. The law said she couldn't be hanged. Why? (Clue: second time lucky)

13. In 1727 George I's hated wife, Dorothea, died. He set off for the funeral but failed to get there. Why? (Clue: a second funeral delayed him)

14. Soon after George I died a raven flew in at the window of his girlfriend, the Duchess of Kendal. She looked after it better than any pet. Why? (Clue: it was something George had crowed about)

15. How can a hot poker cure toothache? (Clue: ear we go again)

16. In 1739 the famous highwayman, Dick Turpin, was

executed. His handwriting was recognized by someone who knew him at school and he was betrayed. Who betrayed Turpin? (Clue: master of treachery)

17. George II and his family ate Sunday dinner in style. What could the public buy on those Sundays? (Clue: feeding time at the zoo?)

18. In the sport of 'Goose Riding' a live goose was hung from a tree branch by its feet. The competitor climbed on a horse. What did he have to do to win? (Clue: the best rider would win by a neck)

19. In 1743 George II became the last British monarch to lead an army into battle at Dettingen, Germany. But his horse disgraced him. How? (Clue: might have made a good race horse)

20. In 1746 James Reid played his bagpipes in York. He never played them again. Why not? (Clue: the noise he made was criminal)

21. In 1747 Lord Lovat became the last person to be beheaded in the Tower of London. As he went to his death 20 other innocent people died. How? (Clue: curiosity killed the cat)

FOUL FOR FEMALES
What was it like for Georgian women? Try this simple test – answer true or false...

1. Georgian women put cork balls in their cheeks to improve their appearance.

2. The average age for women to get married was 15.

3. A woman could be burned alive for murdering her husband.

4. Georgian wives were sometimes sold by their husbands at auction.

5. Men were allowed to beat their wives with sticks.

6. Ladies used cement as make-up.

7. The average wage for a maid was £3 a month.

8. Georgian women often took snuff.

9. A group of Welsh women stopped an invasion by the French.

10. It was fashionable for women to have a sun tan.

WACKY WORDS

Can you match the following Georgian words to their meanings..?

1. grunter	a) idiot
2. hock-docky	b) hangman's noose
3. sumph	c) police constable
4. scrag	d) horse
5. bolly dog	e) shoe
6. big bug	f) eye
7. squeezer	g) shilling coin
8. sad man	h) neck
9. daisy-kicker	i) trouble-maker
10. killer	j) important man

Answers

Quick Georgian Questions

1. Dying. The booklet was burned, so we'll never know how to do this clever trick!

2. He had flogged a pupil until the pupil died. And there are still people today who want to bring back beatings for children. Avoid them.

3. He roasted the boy and ate him. Do not try this with your school dinner ladies, please.

4. They were trying to cure her illness. They also blistered her skin with hot irons and gave her medicines to make her vomit. She died – and was probably glad to go.

5. Anne was so fat she was almost square.

6. She was locked away back in Germany. This was her punishment for flirting with Count Konigsmark. It was worse for the count. He'd been murdered and secretly buried at the castle. Jolly George.

7. He collected the skins of the dogs. He was probably happy to do this because one of his other jobs was to sweep up doggy poo from the streets!

8. He had both hands chopped off.

9. It's said Blackbeard's headless corpse swam round the ship three times before finally sinking!

10. They believed it helped their eyesight.

11. He cut it open to see how an elephant's body works.

12. Because she had been hanged once and pronounced dead. As she was taken off to the graveyard in her coffin she sat up! Lucky Maggie lived another 30 years before dying a second time – for good.

13. George died on his way to the funeral. He had held up Dorothea's funeral for six months. If he'd been quicker he'd have had the pleasure of seeing her put six feet under.

14. George had said that he would visit her after his death. She believed the raven was George. Caw! Imagine that!

15. Burning a hole through the lobe of your ear was supposed to cure the pain in the tooth. Crazy! If you ever see your dentist with a hot poker you know it's time to change dentists.

16. Turpin's school master betrayed him.

17. The public could buy tickets to watch George II and the royal family dine. You could try selling tickets for your neighbours to watch you eat your beans on toast!

18. Grab the head of the goose and tear it off. This was made harder by greasing the goose's beak.

19. As soon as it heard enemy gunfire it ran away. George couldn't stop it! The fat little feller had to go back to his command on foot.

20. He was hanged. The bagpipes were declared 'an instrument of war' after the Scottish Jacobite rebellion of 1745. Happily it is now legal to play these beautiful melodic instruments.

21. Spectators crowded on to wooden stands to watch Lovat get lopped. The stands collapsed and killed 20 people. Served them right.

Foul For Females

1. True.

2. False. The average age was about 24. Very few married under 16.

3. True. But this law was changed in 1789 and the punishment was changed to hanging.

4. True. It wasn't legal but it sometimes happened – and continued to happen until 1887.

5. True. But the stick he used had to be no thicker than his thumb, so that's all right.

6. False. But they did use lead paint, arsenic powder and

plaster of Paris.

7. False. They would be paid about £3 a year.

8. True.

9. True. In 1797 a small group of women from Pembrokeshire, led by Jemima Nicholas, captured 20 men from the invading French. They were so terrifying that the French army surrendered.

10. False. A pale skin was beautiful to the Georgians and women would sometimes wear a mask in front of the face to protect the skin.

Wacky Words
1.g) 2.e) 3.a) 4.h) 5.c) 6.j) 7.b) 8.i) 9.d) 10.f)

INTERESTING INDEX

Where will you find 'pinching competitions', 'squashed fish eyes' and 'stink traps' in an index? In a Horrible Histories book, of course!

Terry Deary was born at a very early age, so long ago he can't remember. But his mother, who was there at the time, says he was born in Sunderland, north-east England, in 1946 – so it's not true that he writes all *Horrible Histories* from memory. At school he was a horrible child only interested in playing football and giving teachers a hard time. His history lessons were so boring and so badly taught, that he learned to loathe the subject. *Horrible Histories* is his revenge.

Martin Brown was born in Melbourne, on the proper side of the world. Ever since he can remember he's been drawing. His dad used to bring back huge sheets of paper from work and Martin would fill them with doodles and little figures. Then, quite suddenly, with food and water, he grew up, moved to the UK and found work doing what he's always wanted to do: drawing doodles and little figures.